The Rehearsal
Pigeon Theatre's Trilogy of Performance Works on Playing Dead

Edited by Anna Fenemore

intellect Bristol, UK / Chicago, USA

First published in the UK in 2012 by Intellect,
The Mill, Parnall Road, Fishponds, Bristol, BS16 3JG, UK

First published in the USA in 2012 by Intellect, The University of Chicago Press,
1427 E. 60th Street, Chicago, IL 60637, USA

Performance permissions: Anyone wishing to perform any of the plays
should contact the heirs to the estates of the playwrights.

A catalogue record for this book is available from the British Library.

Series: Playtext Series
Series editor: Roberta Mock
Series ISSN 1754-0933

Cover designer: Holly Rose
Copy-editor: MPS India
Typesetting: John Teehan
Production Manager: Melanie Marshall

ISBN 978-1-84150-556-5

Printed and bound by Hobbs, UK.

In memory of my father,
Ronald Sidney Fenemore.

And death once dead, there's no more dying then.

Sonnet 146 – Shakespeare

Contents

List of Illustrations

Acknowledgments

Thank you to the School of Performance and Cultural Industries (PCI) at the University of Leeds. Thank you to my colleagues in the former 'Theatre, Dance and Performance' Research Group in PCI for early discussions around the concept of this book: Jonathan Pitches, Tony Gardner, George Rodosthenous, Fiona Bannon and Vicky Hunter. Thanks also to my colleagues Sita Popat, Kara McKechnie, and Jon Brazil.

Thank you to all contributors who were interviewed for the development of the script (see p. 183).

Thank you to Louise Bennett, Martin Buchan, Peter Kennedy, Gillian Knox and Josh Moran for creating these performances, to Amanda Griffkin for producing the work, and to Anna Barzotti and Jim Hinks for their script contributions. Particular thanks to Gillian Knox, whose extensive contribution to the development of these performances was invaluable.

Thank you to Manchester's Performing Arts Network and Development Agency (PANDA) for commissioning the premiere of the trilogy through PANDA-monium, a Manchester Firsts Commission in association with Manchester International Festival 2007. Particular thanks to Liz O'Neill. Thanks also to The Temple of Convenience bar, where the concept for this trilogy was developed, and where the show was first performed.

Thank you to the Arts Council of England for supporting the research and development of *The Rehearsal (a trilogy)* through their Grants for the arts programme (in 2005 for the development of a single show titled *The Rehearsal* (later part 3 of the trilogy), and in 2007 for the development of the whole trilogy).

Thank you to **green**room Manchester, Pigeon Theatre's 'home', where, as associate artists, this trilogy of performances was made. And to **green**room staff: Garfield Allen, Steve Curtis, Ali Dunican, John Franklin, Emma Hardman, Jex Hawksley, Samantha Punt and Tamsin Drury of hÅb. Alas **green**room is no more and will be greatly missed.

Thank you to Kate Fenemore.

Notes on Contributors

Louise Bennett (see **Pigeon Theatre**)

Martin Buchan (see **Pigeon Theatre**)

Alan Fair is Senior Lecturer in Film in the Department of Interdisciplinary Studies, MMU Cheshire, with research interests in Classical American Cinema, Modernist Cinema of Europe, Psychoanalysis and Cinema, Lacanian Psychoanalysis and Cultural Production, and Film, Psychoanalysis and Melancholia.

Anna Fenemore is a lecturer in Theatre and Performance at the School of Performance and Cultural Industries, University of Leeds, specialising in Practice-as-Research, physical performance, site-specific performance and contemporary devised performance. Fenemore's research interests include spectating embodiment, performer bodywork training, multi-sensory immersive performance, performance and phenomenology, theories of performance space/place and performance and death studies. Fenemore is also artistic director of Manchester-based Pigeon Theatre, a contemporary performer and a solo performance artist.

Amanda Griffkin (see **Pigeon Theatre**)

Allan Kellehear is Professor in the School of Health Administration at Dalhousie University in Halifax, Nova Scotia, Canada. He was previously Professor of Sociology and Director of the Centre for Death & Society (CDAS) in the Department of Social and Policy Sciences at the University of Bath, UK. Kellehear's research interests include the history, sociology and social psychology of dying; mystical, religious, altered states associated with dying and bereavement; and public health policies, service sector development, and models for care of dying. He is a member of the Association for the Study of Death & Society (ASDS) and an Academician of the Academy of Social Sciences.

Peter Kennedy (see **Pigeon Theatre**)

Carol Komaromy is a Senior Lecturer and open Media Fellow who joined the Open University in 1994 as a Research Fellow investigating end-of-life care in older people. She has taught and researched in death and dying since then and is well published in this field. Her most recent co-edited book (with Hockey and Woodthorpe) is *The Matter of Death: Space, Place and Materiality*. Carol is one of the members of the Association for Death and Society and co-editor of the international journal, *Mortality*. Her research interests include end-of-life care across the life course and the use of ethnographic methods in sensitive research. Carol's professional background covers nursing, midwifery and counselling.

Gillian Knox (see **Pigeon Theatre**)

Josh Moran (see **Pigeon Theatre**)

Pigeon Theatre are **Anna Fenemore**, **Gillian Knox** and **Amanda Griffkin**. Their practice includes site-specific and studio-based devised contemporary performance works, and the company tours internationally. The company specialise in devised performance work that addresses questions of site-specificity, of non-traditional theatre spaces, of unconventional spatial/social arrangements, and of performer/ spectator intimacy. Gillian Knox has worked as a performer with Pigeon Theatre since 2001. She trained at MMU Cheshire in Contemporary Arts and in Performance Studies at Leeds University. She also works for PickleHerring Theatre as a workshop facilitator and performer/maker. Knox is a lecturer at LIPA and associate lecturer at the University of Leeds. Amanda Griffkin joined the company in April 2007 as producer and, more recently, performer. She trained as a dancer at De Montfort University and also works as a freelance arts project manager and workshop leader. For *The Rehearsal (a trilogy)* Pigeon Theatre worked with Louise Bennett, Martin Buchan, Peter Kennedy and Josh Moran. Louise Bennett studied at MMU Cheshire. Martin Buchan trained at Guildford School of Acting and has extensive experience in theatre and television. Peter Kennedy trained with the Open Performance Centre, Sheffield, and has wide experience of stage, theatre in education and site-specific performance. Josh Moran trained at the Manchester School of Theatre (MMU) and works in theatre, film and television. Pigeon Theatre are UK-based.

Introduction

Anna Fenemore

The *Rehearsal* is a trilogy of site-specific performance texts by Pigeon Theatre, developed from a collaborative, devised process, using verbatim strategies. The works interrogate notions of 'rehearsing death'. Centred around the double meaning of 'playing dead' (the child/adult who 'plays' and the actor who 'plays'), these performance texts and four accompanying critical essays offer readers insights into the interplay between theatrical processes of 'rehearsal' in contemporary performance making and theatrical metaphors of 'rehearsal' in our everyday dealings with trauma, and more specifically, death.

At the outset of the twenty-first century, theories of 'the dying body' have become more and more central to the discussions of social construction and interaction. There is, in the contemporary world, a concern with 'the dying body' that seems to problematise understandings of identity, subjectivity and socialisation, with discourses dealing with trauma, bereavement and the social rituals accompanying death seeming paramount. This book extends these debates through the use of a central theatrical metaphor – rehearsal – which is used strategically at two levels to unpack processes of dying that may occur many years, indeed decades, before death is likely to occur. Firstly, 'rehearsal' as a process where individuals construct imaginatively (through the theatrical processes of projection, playing, pleasure, repetition and composition) scenes of their own and/or their loved ones' deaths and funerals, as a complex means of preparation for (or prevention of) the 'real' (in commonsensical terms) event. Secondly, 'rehearsal' as reference to artistic processes and responses to 'the Real' as trauma (in Lacanian terms):

There's something about imagining it that makes the reality of it not so bad, that means you'll be able to cope with it when it actually happens ... but there's something about when those real experiences happen that you think it's not happening to you, it's happening to someone else, or you're in a film, or you're in a play...

(Gillian in *Happy Hour*)

The shows in *The Rehearsal (a trilogy)* work from scripts composed from two parallel 'rehearsal' activities that evoke the double meaning of 'playing dead':

1. Verbatim interviews: an extensive research period involving the transcription of interviews with around fifty differently aged and gendered individuals on their individual processes of 'rehearsing' for trauma and/or death.

2. Rehearsal documentation: all rehearsals with director and performers (including, significantly, late-night post-rehearsal discussions in the pub) were recorded and transcribed, and this material used verbatim in the script.

Part 1 of the trilogy (*Death Rattle*) is played by two sixty-something men, Part 2 (*Clinging On*) is played by a differently aged/gendered couple and Part 3 (*Happy Hour*) is played by two twenty-something women. The trilogy exposes the commonplace practice of imagining our own deaths and the deaths of others from a dual intention: to prevent it from actually happening; and to prepare oneself for it happening. Simultaneously, in each part of the site-specific trilogy (set in a working bar with food and alcohol served), two performers 'rehearse' for a new show:

In a bar at the end of a long night's drinking two performers collaborate with their audience in the planning and rehearsal of a theatrical performance event. This is a rehearsal of a 'new' show, but also a rehearsal of, and attempt to come to terms with, the inevitability of the death of ourselves and our loved ones.

(*The Rehearsal* publicity)

The action occurs at the tables of the audience, who continue drinking as the show unfurls around and with them, and develops according to the interaction (or not) of the audience, who are invited to play as little or as large a part as they wish. The work is shown through the 'rehearsal' of a script followed by members of the audience that they can comment on and 'improve', whilst also being 'on-script' themselves (playing the parts of Old Man 1, Old Man 2, sound effects operators and prompts). Each performance eventually reveals itself to be its own planning. In this way it ultimately interrogates concepts of 'interactivity', 'collaboration' and 'participation'. The scripts included in this edited book are the basic working scripts used by the company (there are different scripts in Part 2 of the trilogy, where audience members and prompts are given inaccurate scripts strategically). There are points in each of the scripts where the performers improvised around a basic set of ideas, and these points are indicated in the text. The trilogy explores 'rehearsal' as both an imaginative way of approaching (and coming to terms with) death, and as the creative act of preparing/devising/composing theatre. Each show is related to the others around a common theme and structure, but each show comprises a radically different reflection on, and rehearsal of, the processes and potentialities of dying. *The Rehearsal (a trilogy)* was commissioned by, and premiered at, the Manchester International Festival 2007, where it was performed at the Manchester pub The Temple of Convenience.

This book is structured around the three performance texts that make up *The Rehearsal (a trilogy)* (scripts developed by Pigeon Theatre and edited by Anna Fenemore). In the accompanying critical essays four central areas of critical discussion will be introduced by specialists in the following areas: Performance Studies; Sociology; Death Studies/Health and Social Care; and Psychoanalysis and Cultural Theory. The rationale for this juxtaposition between performance text and critical essay is that the essentially 'theatrical' nature of the psychological/sociological/philosophical/medical processes of 'rehearsing death' offers itself to comment/reflection through theatre. Rehearsing death begins to constitute a form of extreme play, and as such is peculiarly pleasurable (this in itself invokes the peculiarly un-pleasurable feeling of guilt):

> For the ultimate limit of play, as all children know, is playing dead. Death is the impossible limit of play because in the landscape of consciousness, in fantasy, in whatever system of representation that we are able to conjure up, it can only ever be played.

> (Quick in Helmer and Malzacher, 2004: 162)

The trilogy of performance texts engages, then, at a creative level with the subject matter, whilst simultaneously operating performatively as a 'rehearsal for death' for potential readers/actors. The accompanying chapters offer critical interrogations of different versions of the 'rehearsal for death' in terms of performative construction (Fenemore), cultural and historical construction (Kellehear), social construction (Komaromy) and the construction of identity and subjectivity (Fair).

In Chapter 1, I offer a contextualisation of Pigeon Theatre's work in the wider tradition of contemporary devised and collaborative performance making as a 'tour' rather than a 'map' (De Certeau, 1985: 122–45), whilst simultaneously offering a discussion of the trilogy and an interrogation of the processes and production of the work and its theoretical frameworks. This chapter articulates concerns surrounding the social impact of imagining death, and makes a connection with Kellehear's (2007) four major stages of the intellectual processes of dying – anticipating, preparing, taming and timing our eventual deaths – through the alignment of these four processes with four specific processes of 'rehearsal' found in much devised performance practice. The chapter goes on to offer a discussion of theatre and performance in relation to notions of belief, exploring the concept of 'belief' as a performative act, as an embodied act and as a subjunctive act.

In *Part 1: Death Rattle*, two sixty-something men towards the end of their double-act career rehearse for an audition showreel for a radio show. Each reflects on the deaths of the people they have loved, the long endurance and hostility of their friendship, and their proximity to death. This is an interactive performance where the audience are invited to act as sound effect operators in the rehearsal for a Radio 4 audition showreel and are on-script throughout.

In Chapter 2, Allan Kellehear offers a critical engagement with the ideas discussed by Fenemore in her chapter. The relationship between the historical emergence of dying behaviour (anticipating, preparing, taming and timing death) and Fenemore's major concepts of artistic rehearsal (anticipation/imagining/projecting, playing/pretence/pleasure, direction/repetition/insistence and editing/*mise-en-scène*/composition) are critically explored. The chapter also provides commentary on the culture-specific nature of dying and performance that may also be part of these theoretical and epistemological reflections.

In *Part 2: Clinging On*, a couple (she in her mid-thirties, he in his early fifties) create multiple imagined scenarios for the death of the other and the end of their relationship, as a way of both coming to terms with the potential loss of, or separation from, their partner, and as a way of somehow preventing that loss/separation. Because of the multitude of imagined scenarios it is unclear whether the process is destructive or affirming. This is an interactive performance where the audience are invited to get into teams and participate in a pub quiz throughout the show.

In Chapter 3, extending Kellehear and Fenemore's fourth categories of timing death and composing performance, Carol Komaromy uses a series of vignettes taken from the experiences of older dying people to explore the idea that death at the end of a long life is more acceptable than death that is considered to be untimely. The vignettes are based on two sets of data, the first from an ethnographic study conducted in care homes for older people in the United Kingdom, which provides different perspectives on what constitutes a good death, and the other from the author's father's period of dying. At the age of seventy, he was not ready to die. The vignette captures some of his turmoil and the way that visions form the Second World War haunted his final months. The chapter will draw on these vignettes to analyse the way in which accounts of dying are socially framed and constructed. Reference is made to the way that Goffman's notion of performance is relevant to achieving a 'good death', however that is interpreted.

In *Part 3: Happy Hour*, two young women (best friends in their mid-twenties) are rehearsing in front of a live audience for a new 'physical theatre' show. The women (in dangerously high heels and getting drunk) imagine the people they love dying dramatically, imagine their own funerals and construct fantasy funeral play-lists and guest-lists, whilst performing risky but impressive and intricate physical choreographies. This is an interactive performance where the audience are invited to stand in as 'characters' in the rehearsal of the 'physical theatre' show and are on-script throughout.

In Chapter 4, Alan Fair concludes this book through a contextualisation of Pigeon Theatre's work in the framework of performance, identity and conceptualisations of the subject. He touches on the rhetoric of life and death: birth is 'a miracle' and death 'a tragedy', and explores what death as a performative 'act' might really signify, with all the meanings that can be attributed to that word (theatrical 'Act', 'acting', 'action'). This chapter proposes that human beings structure works of narrative and durational works of art in a certain way because of our conscious knowledge that life ends in death. As Fair writes: "it is humans who care for beginnings, middles, ends and narratives, not the earth and the stars".

The trilogy in the first instance and this book as a logical extension of that trilogy are an attempt to rehearse for death myself, whilst at the same time being a very personal way of grieving for my dead father, and of coming to terms with my memory of imagining and visualising his death for many years before he actually died. It is also an attempt to justify the peculiar (and somewhat perverse) pleasure I find in imagining my own death and the deaths of those close to me. In finishing this book I find that I am beginning to repeat this curious (and in this context somewhat macabre) practice with my newborn baby daughter, whose 'full-of-life-ness' is deliriously contagious. This work, then, started from a personal need, but anticipates the need for reassurance (that everyone does it) of anyone who has ever imagined the multiple (and 'theatrical') ways in which their father might die, or their daughter, or their mother, lover or son, and anyone who has ever compiled a fantasy funeral play-list, guest-list, eulogy and *mise-en-scène*.

So, I've thought a lot about my own funeral, about everyone being there and it's probably in those times when I'm feeling that, you know, that I need, what's the word? I need kind of reassurance that, you know, I'm loved and that I will be missed. And you can get quite indulgent can't you about imagining everyone being gathered there and their kind of grief at your death? And I get quite carried away to the extent that I'm then disappointed that I'm not actually going to die.

(Louise in *Happy Hour*)

Don't we all want to imagine our own funerals? Those great speeches? The thing is, the catch is, you can't sort of take a bow. And I just kind of wouldn't mind coming back for the bow saying "you bastards why couldn't you say that when I was alive when I could have appreciated it?" There's something that some people say, well actually your mind doesn't disappear for three or four days so imagine actually if you could actually hear all this stuff, "well you've got that wrong, you've got that wrong". I just think it's a hoot: the biggest day of your life you're not there for (well you are there!) [Laughs a lot] It's been fun thinking about these things, it's like an experiment….

(Jonnie in *Clinging On*)

Chapter 1 (Beginnings)

Playing Dead: Rehearsals for Dying

Anna Fenemore

W e often speak of mapping the performance space, or of mapping our pasts or our futures. Drawing on de Certeau's distinction between 'space' and 'place' and between 'map' and 'tour' (1984: 115–30), this chapter argues that the 'tour' is the basic nature of the process of rehearsing, and is simultaneously the basic nature of our everyday experience of 'rehearsing' in the present. This everyday rehearsal manifests itself primarily as the repetitive reconstruction of what might have been in the past, and as the incessant imagination/projection of what might be in the future.

I used to imagine winning Wimbledon or being a really talented musician or a singer in a band. I imagined being a singer and being an actress. I used to imagine my house catching on fire. I imagined road accidents before I went anywhere. I imagined meeting this wonderful man. I imagined my parents dying over and over again and I still do ... I imagine my sister and her husband dying in a car crash and I have to look after their children for the rest of their lives as if they were my own.

(Anna in *Clinging On*)

This chapter reflects on *The Rehearsal (a trilogy)* through exploring the concept of 'rehearsing' as both theatrical term and as metaphor denoting our everyday processes of imaginative fantasy that are an (often invisible, unmarked or un-remarked upon) attempt to come to terms with the inevitability of the death of ourselves and our loved ones.

The Rehearsal (a trilogy) is a trilogy of site-specific theatre performances that interrogate notions of 'rehearsing death' as forms of dark or deep play, where "death and playing are inextricably linked" (Quick in, 2004: 162). The work begins to ask questions across and between differently aged and gendered individuals about the everyday and commonplace practice of imagining our own and others' deaths. This might be as some kind of preparation for the 'real' thing, or as some kind of strategy for preventing these things from happening, or as a way of somehow making mundane the traumatic moments (whether real or imagined) of our lives where we come face-to-face with death and dying. The trilogy also begins to establish resonances across and between the imaginative process of 'rehearsing' for death/ trauma and the creative process of 'rehearsing' for theatre/performance. With this dual articulation of 'rehearsal', this chapter offers an interrogation of 'rehearsing death' and 'rehearsing theatre' as forms of dark or deep play that engage with differing types of 'belief' (specifically exploring the concept of 'belief' as performative, embodied and subjunctive act).

In *A Social History of Dying*, Kellehear (2007) outlines four major challenges of dying, and throughout this chapter I will be making connections between Kellehear's four challenges (1. anticipating, 2. preparing, 3. taming, and 4. timing our eventual deaths) and the four processes that I propose to be the central processes of artistic 'rehearsal' in devised performance practice (1. anticipation, imagination and projection, 2. playing, pretence and pleasure, 3. direction, repetition and/or insistence, 4. editing, *mise-en-scène* and composition), and will illustrate these with the stories of 'playing dead' told by contributors to the trilogy performance project. As themes or tropes, Kellehear's four challenges can be seen weaving through the chapter, in both the reflections on the processes of artistic 'rehearsal' and in the reproduction here of contributors' interviews/stories. Some of these stories might be found directly in the scripts included in this volume (where this is the case, readers are directed to the appropriate character and playtext), and other stories that were not included in the final scripts, but are useful here, are also included in the text. These stories from contributors' interviews are made anonymous, though a list of contributors is included at the end of the book. These stories will be italicised.

Kellehear makes it very clear in his book that the four major challenges of dying exist as dominant, rather than entirely mutually exclusive, challenges of four different historical/social/temporal eras (respectively: Stone Age, Pastoral, Urban and Cosmopolitan). For Kellehear, these four categories are not fixed exclusively into these periods and may bleed across and between ages, "all challenges within the act of dying can be found in all periods and places in history" (2007: 234) (as the four processes of artistic 'rehearsal' also remain uncertain and 'bleeding'). It is important to note here that Kellehear makes it very clear that the four stages he writes about are not mutually exclusive, nor are they chronologically exclusive. The same can be said for the processes of rehearsal I outline here, where different directors or different collaborative groups have different chronologies of working. *Mise-en-scène* might, for example, be the first thing that happens, or playing and pretence might simultaneously be used with composition. Needless to say, the identification and subsequent categorisation of these different rehearsal processes have come primarily from my work as director and performer with Pigeon Theatre and are, of course, always subject to 'bleeding'.

1. Anticipation, imagination and projection (or 'anticipating death')

Anticipating death may have been central to all our major political, economic, spiritual and scientific development. In this way, society has not been built to shield us from death but rather to help us anticipate and prepare us for death's quite specific challenges. Against the humorous contemporary observation that life is no rehearsal is the more sober counter-observation from prehistory that it may very well be just that. Life – as personal and social development in society – may indeed originally have been viewed as a rehearsal for the challenges of the otherworld journey.

(Kellehear, 2007: 54)

For Kellehear, the challenge of 'Anticipating Death' dominates the Stone Age, where communities anticipate collectively the journey into and through the other world. In the Stone Age, hunter-gatherers, whose deaths were often unexpected, violent and early, did not see life and death, or 'this world' and 'other world', as "sharply separate types of existence" (Kellehear, 2007: 7), instead 'dying' was seen as a post-death journey (2007: 16). In life the challenge was to anticipate that journey into the other world and hence be prepared for its "inevitable tests" (2007: 7). Collectively such a challenge demanded an element of imaginative thinking and projecting into the future – the other world journey is unknown and as such there were the anticipatory responses of desiring to

predict the coming of death; the desire to ward it off; the desire to identify the risks of encountering it ... the desire to learn more about it; the desire to prepare for it; and the desire to plan around it.

(Kellehear, 2007: 47–8)

Elements of anticipation, imagination and projection can be seen vividly in the stories and the scripts in this volume, but can also be seen as a process engaged in by performance makers, often as the beginnings of the process of creation. Performance makers (to varying degrees) anticipate their audience, imagine final 'products' and both project into the future (in terms of seeing the future of a performance) and also project themselves (depending on the style of theatre) into characters, situations and/or *potential* relationships with their *potential* audiences. And this stage of performance making is mostly unsettled, open-ended and terrifying:

I guess I tend to rehearse these things in quite an instinctive way but there is a sense in which I am terrified at the beginning of the process because I don't really have a plan but experience has taught me that the best work or the best results have come from engaging with that terror and seeing what happens. The more experience I have the more frightened I become ironically. In some senses the more successful a rehearsal process has been the more pressure it puts onto the next time.

(Louise in *Happy Hour*)

Remembering my father's deaths

When my father died I remembered the multiple ways in which I had imagined him dying before that. I became aware of the endless versions I had anticipated, imagined and projected of his death – some gory, some gentle, some dramatic, some mundane. I should mention that my father, who I was very close to, had been ill for much of my life. After his death it took me a few months before my guilt about these imagined scenarios, or death-scenes (to use a theatrical metaphor), allowed me to talk with others about this practice. At this point it became clear that whilst I thought this to be a perverse, inexcusable and unacceptably curious act, it was in fact a common, if not everyday, practice undertaken by many people as a way of taking control over a number of different areas of their lives, but particularly in relation to death: the death of ourselves and our loved ones.

It's something that I talk about a lot actually and I know why I do it. It's because my father died when I was four and I've worked out why I do it. And I also do it coz I'm quite good at visualisation so um how do I do it? So I find a partner that I want to spend the rest of my life with, I go out with that partner, I marry them and I imagine that they will die when my youngest child is four years old and the reason I do that is that I'm the youngest child in my family and my father died when I was four. And my mother was the youngest child in her family and her father died when she was four years old. So at some level I think I'm cursed. And at another level I absolutely know that that isn't going to happen, but there's something about imagining it that makes the reality of it somehow not so bad, … so I kind of imagine I suppose what would be a worse case scenario, so my son who's three, I imagine what would happen if nursery phoned me up or my husband phoned me up or I went upstairs and found him dead in bed. And part of me knows that that is a real possibility so … um … so I try to … I try to … just imagine what I would feel … and … when I imagine it I don't feel any terror or horror, I'm quite calm in the situation and I'm dealing with it. So I guess at

*some level I'm kind of planning the best case response I might have in that situation …
um ….*

(Anna in *Clinging On*)

Touring memory and imagined futures

The site-specific nature of these performance works is a deliberate strategy for linking
the two modes of 'playing dead' articulated here (artistic rehearsal and imaginative
everyday 'rehearsals' for the future). Through allowing the works to unfold as a 'tour'
(as site-specific work tends to do) rather than a 'map', and allowing alternative modes of
visuality to operate in the performance environments of these works, readers/viewers
are reminded of the fundamental nature of our everyday imaginings of the future,
which constitute a *tour* through imagined spaces and imagined memories and futures,
rather than a *map*. The concept of 'tour' and 'map' are here derived from de Certeau
(1985). De Certeau's concept of a 'map' (1985: 122–45) refers to the visual ordering
of elements and is a *pictorial* field composed of elements ordered according to visual
relationships of coexistence. The 'map' features spectatorial distance, objectification
and a frontal point of view. On the other hand de Certeau's concept of a 'tour' (1985:
122–45) refers to the instability and multiple possibilities of intersections between
elements moving in time, and is therefore a *vectorial* field created by the movements
used within it. The 'tour' demands that the eyes orient the viewer to the world in
terms of their physical place in it and allows viewers to experience *situation* and
momentum. In negotiating our memories and imagining our futures we are never
merely mapping them out according to de Certeau's definition of a 'map'. Instead these
scenarios reference either something we have lived through or something that we
potentially might live through, but more importantly we live through the memory
of them (as research into how memory works has started to discover – memory is
recreated anew every time we remember it, rather than existing as a snapshot (or
'map') of a moment in time that is somewhere 'stored' in the brain for future retrieval,
see Lehrer 2007 for an overview). These might be 'real' or simply imagined memories,
ones we have created for ourselves from the stories of others, or they may be like
my very first memory (a pigeon flying above a skylight), which I no longer think I
really remember. I remember remembering it, I remember telling my parents that
I remember it, I remember them talking about when it might have been, but I do
not really remember it – it is an imagined scenario, a faded memory stuck together
or patched together through a family's insistent storytelling. Imagined memories
such as these are much like the imagined scenarios that we develop in response to
badly managed situations – the constant argument I have in my head with my noisy

neighbours and their noisy dog. The witty put-down we only think of after the event, the argument that should have been (and not the one that actually was). And these two different forms of reconstruction of the past (the imagined or reconstructed memory, and the rehearsed and thus bettered past) are much like the imagined scenarios that we create for ourselves for our futures, often (though of course not exclusively) related to trauma, to death. These negotiations of past (including 'real' memory) and future cannot claim to be 'maps' in de Certeau's sense (pictorial, distanced, objectified and with a frontal point of view), rather they are 'tours' in de Certeau's sense (vectorial, immediate, subjectified and with an orientation determined by the physical position of the subject inside the experience).

In short, and perhaps like those in the Stone Age anticipating death, these imagined pasts and futures do not exist as a visual map, but as a concrete physical tour – we are not outside them looking in, we are inside them looking out. Our real and imagined pasts and our imagined futures are tours (in the same way that our experience of space in the everyday is marked by the experience of the tour) in that the self in all these constructs is constituted as both observer and observed, subject and object, passive and active, just like our everyday lived experience. We are inside these imaginations/memories and we experience situation and momentum – we get carried away, we get frightened, we find perverse pleasure in the process of imagining, and we are part of a wider corporeal field (where we may be both physically and emotionally moved: thrilled, saddened, horrified, delighted and so on). But most importantly we do not have a controlling relationship, a spectatorial distance or a frontal point of view towards these imagined or remembered scenarios. Instead we are embedded in the past and the future and when we imagine our loved ones dying we do not know if we do it to control the future or to prevent things from happening or to prepare ourselves for its happening.

In a sense you never live in the present you always live in some kind of idea of the future or trapped by some memory of the past so it's all a rehearsal in that sense. I run through scenarios in my head, I hope such and such is OK today when I meet him, I hope, if they're junkies, they're not too stoned, or if they're alcoholics, I hope they're not drunk, or if they're grumpy, I hope they're not too fucking grumpy. Life is always about rehearsal. It's supposed to be spontaneous, that's bollocks, it's all rehearsed. Everything is always planned. Do you know what I mean? That's why things can happen to us and surprise us, oh I didn't plan for that or this, precisely because we plan for everything that can happen. That's what we do every day, we get up in the morning and we start planning. Do you know what I mean? Sometimes you can be having a conversation with someone in a bar and you're not even listening because you're planning what you're going to say next. Do you know what I mean?

(part of this story is used by Jonnie in *Clinging On*)

2. Playing, pretence and pleasure (or 'preparing for death')

[O]f course when I start thinking about it and think oh no I haven't really made any preparations and there are things that I wouldn't really want people to find, private letters and diaries and just having your stuff in order and I often think, oh gosh should I always have everything in order just in case? Should I get my things in order? Or leave a letter with someone who is very close to me with instructions and a set of keys you know [laughs]? So, I suppose metaphorically it sometimes feels a bit like swimming in at the deep end, knowing that you can swim, but also knowing that it's very hard to tread water for long periods of time and stay afloat.

(Louise in *Happy Hour*)

OK – so my death scene would go something like this – I'd be lying in her arms and I'd say: "The whole point is I know I've often seemed somewhat detached but can I make it plain, how deeply and how wonderfully I have been so much in love with you. That my love for you has no bounds. Not very romantic I know. My love for you has no equal". This doesn't sound as good as I wanted it to. Then I'd die.

(part of this story is used by Jonnie in *Clinging On*)

In the Pastoral Age, Kellehear argues that the dominant challenge of dying was one of preparing for death. Early Settlement cultures began to see longer life cycles and the people were more likely to see death coming. Death became a 'this world' as well as 'other world' activity, and began to be much more of a personal as well as collective experience. For the first time, in the Pastoral society, it was not just survivors that could engage in preparing for (or anticipating) death, but now so too could those people who were actually dying, and they could begin to make their own preparations for a 'good death' (2007: 83):

When people with possessions began to take time to die, most of them used that time to prepare. But why … don't people just walk away from their social responsibilities and look to enjoy the last hours, days or weeks? Why, when time is so obviously precious, do we spend it in preparations, in busying ourselves in a kind of administrative spirit of social transfer? Why, when dying eventually became a this-world affair, did it get suddenly co-opted into tasks and obligations? Why do the dying do this? What's in it for them?

(Kellehear, 2007: 106)

Preparing for death or getting one's things in order as a theme or trope recurs over and over again in the interviews Pigeon Theatre conducted. Acts such as these are attempts to be in control of something that is fundamentally uncontrollable, but in the process a 'better' outcome might be achieved. What these acts perhaps even more importantly do is 'try things out' before they will happen 'for real'. In performance-making terms the acts of playing, pretence and pleasure do precisely this. They open up areas of uncertainty through their attempt to make discoveries or challenge oneself. They prepare the actor/performer for the unexpected, for the unfamiliar, for the uncertain, but most importantly they allow the performance maker the opportunity to 'try things out' during a rehearsal phase that is generally exploratory, improvisatory, open, unfixed, unstriated and marked by imaginative acts. The imagining of trauma in our everyday lives is also a mark of either 'getting prepared' such that we are in a state of readiness, or it acts as a 'charm' whereby we might avoid it.

OK, well, my favourite death fantasy today: I'm heroically walking to my car, being struck down by lightning, and being taken away in an ambulance. After imagining my death, my mind flashes to the funeral. I see my friends gathered round, and you, mourning my modest (but heroic) life. I have at least one death fantasy a day. And while they all share an identical ending, it's profoundly satisfying to vary the mode of death. I can't recall whether I've ever been struck by lightning before. This might be a first. We were on a flight and the speaker on the aeroplane said there was a fire in the toilet. We did an emergency landing and you said 'how did you stay so calm?' and I said I was prepared, if this is the end, so be it. And I certainly rehearse those things over and over as a way of preparing myself, but also sometimes as a way of stopping it from happening. I tend to do it when I'm on my own and when I should be doing a very ordinary thing like washing up or feeding the cat but I'm not. I'm filling time with fantasies of me dying, of you dying.

(Anna in *Clinging On*)

Dark and deep play

If we were to begin to theorise these imaginative acts, then an appropriate model would be that of play theory, specifically 'deep' and 'dark' play, in relation to the practice of imagining the traumas of one's future. In particular, I'm interested in Caillois (2001), Ackerman (1999) and Schechner's (2002) accounts of play theory, and also Hind's (2010) account of dark and deep play in the performance arena. Schechner has defined dark play as involving fantasy, risk, luck, daring, invention and deception. Dark play may be entirely private, known to the player alone or can erupt suddenly, a bit of micro play, seizing the player(s) and then as quickly subsiding – a wisecrack, burst of frenzy, delirium, or deadly risk … Dark play subverts order, dissolves frames and breaks its own rules and the gratification and thrill of dark play involves physical risk-taking to invent new selves to engage one's inner self to communion with the other. There is something excitingly liberating about this kind of playing.

(Schechner, 2002: 106–7)

Dark play, whilst being a particularly subversive activity, is fundamentally a conscious act that can lead into what might be termed 'deep play'. I am here following Hind's (2010) definition of deep play as "the mode of playing a person achieves whilst in the midst of playing itself" (2010: 15). Hind follows Ackerman's description of deep play as

the ecstatic form of play. In its thrall, all the play elements are visible, but they're taken to intense and transcendent heights. Thus deep play should really be classified by mood, not activity. It testifies to *how* something happens, not *what* happens.

(Ackerman, 1999: 12, my italics)

Deep play in this definition has much to do with the rewards and pleasures associated with risk-taking. But Ackerman's assertion that deep play should be classified by mood, and not activity, implies that deep play can also occur in the mundane and the 'low-risk', with the action split from the attitude. What should be considered here is that it "is the player's motivation, mood, attitude and engagement [within the play] that render the activity 'deep' and rewarding" (Hind, 2010: 15), and not the activity itself. The focus on deep play as *how* something is done rather than *what* is done reveals deep play as a fundamentally performative act. Or at least it exists liminally somewhere *between* the unconscious or ecstatic act and the conscious or performative act. In this way the notion of 'deep play' as a performative act of mundanity is one that is of particular interest to me as a performance maker – where performance makers are routinely expected to explore the performance acts of the extraordinary or as Barba terms it, the 'extra-daily' (Barba and Savarese, 1991), as opposed to the 'every-daily'.

I think about my own death a lot. An image that I have, have had for years, is a sniper getting me … The sniper is what I'm dodging, the sniper is like me presenting my annual accounts, I've dodged another year, nobody's caught me out, Newton is my middle name, I haven't succumbed to gravity, I'm still flying. There's no reason I should do. Like the bumblebee, my continuing existence cannot be accounted for by science, I should have fallen to the ground. But the sniper hasn't got me even though I am in his sights. I actually see me in his sights, I feel the sights strangle me, I feel the gun barrel moving somewhere in the distance as I'm walking in the street and it still doesn't get me.

(Jonnie in *Clinging On*)

In making *The Rehearsal (a trilogy)* there was something significant about two areas of the everyday. First, there was the idea of *mundanity* and the everyday. Thinking about dying, our own dying and the deaths of those whom we love, is not the *extra*ordinary act I had thought it to be when I first began reflecting on what I was doing in relation to my father's death(s). Rather it is an ordinary or everyday act for many people, and is therefore a mundane act of seemingly little dramatic interest or 'performance-worthiness'. Second, there was the idea of *terror* and the everyday. Tim Etchell's idea of "[y]ou play with what scares you" (1999: 59) operates both at the level of the everyday and through the creative act of making theatre.

There's a two aspect thing, there's an imagining it that means you will be able to cope when it happens, but there's also the fear that if you imagine it too much you're going to bring it on so that really weird thing where you're thinking thoughts and you're thinking actually ... and also psychologically I'm aware that you can bring things on in the sense that I've often envisaged lots of really positive things happening and imagined myself into jobs or into relationships or into ... and those things have happened. So because those things have happened I know they've not just happened because I've imagined them but I'm also aware that it could work the other way round, that if I think hard and strong enough about it, I could actually bring about the deaths of my loved ones. And I'm not sure what to do with that. It's a strange one actually.

(Louise in *Happy Hour*)

Playing dead

We are unable to manage death and any attempt to 'know' it remains deliciously out of reach. The devastating and liberating effect of embracing the terror that death produces is that it unhinges the systems of representation binding the subjects together. This unbinding of the subject puts the mind (and body) into a state of disequilibrium, in a state of flux and play. And it is here that the 'now', the child-like encounter, the extreme limits of possibility may be experienced … death and playing are inextricably linked.

(Quick in Helmer and Malzacher, 2004: 157–62)

The first time I played dead was as a child in the game 'sleeping lions'; I played it again a few years ago with my then six-year-old niece when she came into my bedroom earlier than I would have wished and asked to play – I agreed to a game of sleeping lions, crept back under the covers and dozed luxuriously whilst congratulating myself on my cleverness, as she 'played' at being dead seriously. As she 'played dead', it was 'as if' I were playing dead.

'As if': The subjunctive – what is imagined, or wished, or possible. A 'temporary acceptance' of an imaginary universe. A performative act. A pretence. An act designed to make possible and accessible a certain kind of belief in theatre.

Pretending to be dead and other acts of believing

I do not remember when I stopped believing in Father Christmas, and neither does my younger sister. My mother does not know when we stopped believing and whilst being close to my father I never had that conversation with him (though as I was thirty-two when he died, I expect he knew that I knew that it was really him). There was no playground denouement, no horrified demands for confirmation of existence to my mother, no ridiculing of my younger sister for still believing. And I do not think I am alone in this. I think there are many children who continue behaving *as if* Father Christmas really exists without ever considering why they continue with this performative behaviour, or even acknowledging that they do so. I continued investing in a proposition: Father Christmas, and behaved 'as if' he were true. As de Certeau suggests, 'belief' is a performative act in that it is not

> the object of believing (a dogma, a program, [Father Christmas] etc.) but … the subject's investment in a proposition, the act of saying it and considering it as true – in other words, a "modality" of the assertion and not its content.

(de Certeau, 1984: 178)

So 'belief' in these terms is a subject's investment in a proposition, a performative act, a pretence, my own juvenile investment in the proposition of Father Christmas, a performer's investment in the moment of performance, a spectator's performative act of believing in the moment of performance, and believing in the pretence.

21

For de Certeau, then, there is a distinction between the 'modality' of an assertion, and its 'content'. So whilst it could be argued that we can no longer believe in something again after we know it to be otherwise (Father Christmas), this only accounts for the content of the assertion (there is no Father Christmas), it does not account for the modality of the assertion (behaving *as if* there were a Father Christmas). The difficulty in using the term 'belief' in discussing performance comes when we focus on content rather than modality, and 'belief' in much of the training language of theatre orthodoxy persists as an emotional or psychological engagement with an 'object of believing' ('truth', character, situation, circumstance, subtext). But where belief is a capacity to sustain an imagined or apprehended performance object (character or situation), even when it is known that the object has no existence independent of the 'work' of performance, something other than the intellectual knowledge of the existence of that object must be going on. As Zarrilli asserts in *Acting (Re)Considered*:

[t]he language of "believability" is problematic because ... this particular metaphor ... "believe" is devoid of any reference to the body; there is no assertion that "believability" needs to be embodied.

(Zarrilli, 1995: 9)

Belief might therefore be (re)configured here and now, no longer metaphor, but as embodied, performative act. And, if belief is understood as a performative and embodied act or set of behaviours (rather than either an acceptance of an object of belief, or an intellectual or psychological investment in a proposition), with a version of this unique to performance work, then the subjunctive is the central modality of performance belief systems. The subjunctive: that which is imagined or wished or possible. For a spectator and a performer it is *as if* certain things are.

And this reminds me of my changing relationship with Father Christmas, in which there existed three overlapping and indistinguishable phases (in what is precisely the same altering relationship many people have to God) – belief as knowledge (there is a Father Christmas/God) – belief as performative act (behaving *as if* there is a Father Christmas/God) – and non-belief (there is no Father Christmas/God). 'Belief' in theatre occupies that second, performative, subjunctive and embodied, phase – behaving *as if* certain things are. This subjunctive mode is very clearly seen in performance's relationships to time and space. For example, actors in realist/naturalist work behave *as if* they were not in the same space and time as the audience. In much contemporary devised performance it could be argued that performers behave *as if* they were in the same space and time as their audience (direct address for example seems to refer to the actual audience there at that time and in that space, but is, of course, merely a repetition of a rehearsed speech/score). Actors in fictional, representational theatre pretend to be someone else, they behave *as if* they were someone else, and audiences behave *as if* they believed them. Invariably, physical performance training regimes teach students to relocate bodily states concretely in the body through a realignment or allocation of tensions. In the West such training regimes (e.g. ballet) cover up the work done ('tame' it), in an attempt to 'fictionalise' (or 'heroise' or 'mythologise') performers' bodies, in the same way that traditional, narrative or naturalistic western performance 'fictionalises' performers' bodies through disguise (*pretending* to be exhausted, in pain etc.). The first style of performer training therefore encourages the performer to 'show less' whilst the second to 'show more'. These modes of 'more' or 'less' perpetuate a world of the subjunctive *as if* in the performer.

What this subjunctive nature of belief demonstrates is that the content of believing (audience in same space and time as performers, for example) can be separated from the activity or modality of believing (behaving *as if* audience are not in the same space and time). In religion for many people there is a moment in their relationship to God that is a performative act of deep play. And in theatre (particularly in highly fictional modes of representational theatre, but also to varying degrees in other kinds of theatre), belief is performative in that we propose the subjunctive, what is imagined, or wished or possible, as performance makers, and as spectators we undertake a 'temporary acceptance' of an imaginary universe. The act of rehearsing death in our everyday lives is similarly a subjunctive act. We pretend to die, we play at dying, it is *as if* we die. And we get a certain amount of pleasure from this. We undertake a temporary acceptance of an imaginary universe, one that no longer contains us.

3. Direction, repetition and/or insistence (or 'taming death')

For Kellehear, urban development encouraged a new challenge for dying – that of taming death, of making it manageable, and in particular of bringing in professionals, or those that know better, to manage death for you. With the arrival of the city came the

> social habit of finding others to do one's work or to supply one with services that might alter or improve important social experiences such as birth, illness, work or death … Three professionals were important for helping to transform the good death of the Pastoral Age to an experience managed, or at least share-managed, but others who were not directly kith or kin. These were the doctor, the priest and the lawyer.
>
> (Kellehear, 2007: 131)

The managed death here is a tamed death, taming the "chaos and uncertainty of impending death" (2007: 7). Likewise in the rehearsal processes of contemporary devised performance work, there is a need (for many companies and artists) at some point to 'tame the chaos and uncertainty' of playing, pretence and pleasure, and for the openness of preparations/devising materials/playing to be 'tamed'. It is here that a director perhaps steps in to begin to shape material and to work closely with performers from the position of 'outside' and to begin to 'tame' the 'wild' behaviour of playing, pretence and pleasure.

Similarly other modes of 'striation' can begin to be applied to the process, in particular repetition and/or 'insistence', a word used by Gertrude Stein to counter accusations that her work was repetitive, and a word that might more usefully describe the 'repetitions' of performance:

> About "repetition" and "insistence" Stein spoke at length in "Portraits And Repetition". Repetition, of course, is what she had been charged with over and over by resistant, uncomprehending readers. She says that human beings do not repeat themselves, for if they are alive, their emphasis is different with every statement, every movement. This is insistence.

> (Dydo, 2003: 621)

Actors are regularly required to play the unplayable, to represent the unrepresentable, to know the unknowable, and the way they do this is through a number of different methods: imagining what it might be like if …; trying out different and multiple ideas, scenarios, solutions etc; acknowledging the ordinary through the extraordinary; approaching the subject through an attitude rather than through actually doing it (that is, dying, killing someone etc); conducting the performative action rather than the 'real' action (in proceeding through the *act* of doing it, rather than *actually* doing it); but most significantly they do it through the (less exciting?) act of *insistence*. And this is precisely what we do in the everyday when we imagine our own deaths and the deaths of others. We rehearse, try out, acknowledge the ordinary and mundane nature of death through the ordinary (yet curiously perverse) process of endlessly imagining it, and we approach the subject through an attitude rather than an action, through an 'act' rather than through a 'real' action. But most of all we repeat it, over and over, until we end up either with multiple versions (my father's many imagined deaths, or the many different death stories told by Louise and Gillian in *Happy Hour*, or the many versions of Anna's own death in *Clinging On* – her favourite today: being struck by lightning), or with the 'perfect' single version (Peter's sixty-fifth birthday repeated over and over as an attempt to dodge fate in *Death Rattle*, or Jonnie's ideal death scene in *Clinging On*).

I'll tell you something about rehearsal. In book three of Francois Rabelais' four-book epic Gargantua *and* Pantagruel, *there features a scamp called Panurge. In the third book, Panurge wants to get married, and Panurge basically rehearses in his mind all the possible scenarios for marriage such that he can actually never get married, and it reminds me of ... getting a little bit, stupidly philosophical, but I think it's Nietzsche who talks about rather than doing the thing – getting married – you think about it. Nietzsche says if you do not take action then all the energy that would have been used in that action retroverts so that in other words, all your time spent training, spent rehearsing an event you will probably never do, it starts feeding itself in a kind of, well it's very generative but what it generates is ever more sort of, I can use the sense, I don't mean this, I was going to use the word crippled, you can use it or not, but ever more crippled narratives, narratives that defeat the possibility of action or of things happening and everything is coming back on yourself, you start eating yourself through the repeated rehearsal of the action that finally never takes place. But is being continually narrated as if it were. And the better it is rehearsed, the better it is performed as narrative, the less likely it is it will ever happen. Do you see that funny backward stepping? And Panurge is the perfect example of that. That his anguish at the risk of taking that leap into the unknown, into being with another person, means that he just makes up all these marriage stories. So if you think it through it won't happen, if you keep thinking about it and keep rehearsing it and repeating it over and over again, and this is a really interesting model to think about – you must know lots of people whose lives are filled with those failed negotiations, around that failed event, which in their imagination they have heroically accomplished but everybody knows they haven't done. But they've imagined it over and over so often, they've repeated it so often to themselves that it becomes real.*

(Contributor story)

4. Editing, *mise-en-scène* and composition (or 'timing death')

Kellehear argues that the dominant form of dying in the Cosmopolitan Age is a long dying, a shameful dying and/or dying in old age; "long dying produces journeys of dying that are extremely difficult, testing and stigmatising" (2007: 207). This dying is one that also has the most formal organisational or institutional control – decisions now are made for individuals by huge national or international institutions (health care providers, governments). There is an "erosion of awareness of dying ... erosion of support for dying ... [and the] problem of stigma" (2007: 210–11) in particular linked to dying at a very old age, or dying before one's time. Kellehear positions the final challenge, therefore, as a challenge of timing.

The problem of the "right" time to die has been a growing concern of the Twentieth Century but the demographic swell of ageing that will peak in the Twenty-First Century of the Cosmopolitan Age will see this become the major challenge for dying in the future.

(Kellehear, 2007: 233)

Kellehear goes on to answer "when is the right time to die?" with "Before or After" (2007: 236). Before it is too late, and after it is too soon. The challenge is one of timing, but to use a more theatrical/musical term, it is also one of 'composition'. Composition, as an artistic tactic for placing things in the right place and at the right time in a work of art, therefore clearly has connotations of editing and of *mise-en-scène*. Choosing what and when to place something within the frame of theatre is arguably the final challenge of contemporary devised work.

I tend to describe my preferred style of rehearsal as fast and dirty. And what I generally mean by that is that most of the decisions I make about what ends up in the final product is very much made in the space, in the moment, in terms of bringing all the varying materials that I have been … all the research materials into the space and then animating them in some way and seeing how one image might connect to a piece of text, might connect to a conceptual idea and have some sort of meaning for me that I like in that moment.

(Louise in *Happy Hour*)

Of course, in *The Rehearsal (a trilogy)*, much of the compositional, editorial and *mise-en-scène* decisions were made in terms of the site-specificity of the work, and in so doing these decisions further enabled this work to act as 'tour' and not 'map' for all participants (performers and spectators). This is curious, since the processes of composition, editing and *mise-en-scène* might themselves be seen as processes of 'mapping'. But their *affect* is one of 'touring'. The simplest way to write about these decisions is to write about the final performance's *affect* (since all editing, *mise-en-scène* and compositional decisions were made with this in mind). In *The Rehearsal (a trilogy)* there is no design (beyond its site-specificity), there are no props (beyond the beers, cake and sandwiches given out to the audience), there are no beautiful visual images created. Each show is ostensibly just two people talking in a bar (much like the late night post-rehearsal drinks that constituted much to the development of this particular work, but also, I would argue, that constitute an important part of the making process of others' performance work). There is, therefore, a sense of visual detachment (there is often nothing to look at) and even more significantly there is an extreme physical

26

intimacy between performer and spectator. The performers sit at the tables in the bar with the spectators, they chat together, play in teams together for the pub quiz in *Clinging On,* spectators take on roles in the work, they are on script, they can speak, interact, participate, get drunk with the performers. There is something about the use of synchronous space, and in particular intimate, immersive space such as the bar in *The Rehearsal,* that allows for different types of visual engagement with the work – in particular what might be termed 'haptic' potential, from Deleuze and Guattari, who write of 'haptic' potential as the visual sense of touch that interpenetrates visual and physical space (1988: 492–3). What occurs with the haptic is a looking that goes *beyond* vision; here there is not simply a *threat* that a performer can touch a spectator, moments of haptic vision instead offer a closeness and spatial inclusion that in the everyday is regulated by certain ethical rules. These elements of an alternative mode of visuality (one that relies on haptic vision) ensure that the spectator (as well as the performer) cannot get sufficiently outside the work in order for them to have a concrete optical option for mapping out the space. They are too close to and too visually detached from the work to be able to create a map of it. Instead they inhabit it and transgress between spectator and participant, social group and individual, object and subject, on-looker and looked-upon. The person who is looking is also being looked at. Such a transgressional inhabitation of space is routine in the everyday where we continually cross over between social and local, between your world and mine, between subject and object and between optical space and haptic space. *The Rehearsal (a trilogy)* attempts to bring this multimodal perceptual experience of everyday transgressional inhabitation into the performance arena. This mode of inhabitation is achieved through an interweaving of spectating bodily/visual space and performing bodily/visual space, where participants are 'in the world' together as individuals are in the everyday.

In a curious subversion of what we might commonly understand to be the objectivity of the map and the subjectivity of the tour, what is happening here (through editing, *mise-en-scène* and composition) is that the spectator is affected by finding pleasure in her role as object – that which is looked at, intended towards, spoken to. She has not disappeared into the blackness of the auditorium or the anonymity of 'as if' she were not there, where her primary role would be as subject observing the performing objects ahead of her. Instead, she too has also become object in her experience of the work as a tour through imagined spaces and imagined memories and imagined futures.

Endings

It is clear for me that the experiences of rehearsing and of performing, as complex and multilayered articulations of actions in time, more accurately fits de Certeau's (1984) definition of 'space' than 'place', of 'tour' than 'map'. In "Practices of Space" (de Certeau, 1985) we witness the pedestrian who uses spaces that she herself cannot see, for which she has no knowledge from above; instead the pedestrian moves along and effectively creates a path that intertwines with other paths and that spatialises the city rather than being contained within it or prescribed by it. In a similar way the process of rehearsing (in spite of how clear a brief there is or objectives or desires) is always a process of 'touring' rather than 'mapping', where those involved do not necessarily have an overview. Instead they are 'immersed' in multiple processes of anticipation, imagining, projecting, playing, pretence, pleasure, direction, repetition, insistence, and it is not until the stage of editing and *mise-en-scène* and composition that any real sense of 'mapping' the work (in terms of fixing it or 'placing' it) comes about, and even then that process of 'placing' the work might, as is the case in *The Rehearsal (a trilogy)*, be a strategy for allowing spectators to 'tour' the work. And the significant thing here is that rehearsing (like 'touring') may well have a sense of the overarching intention of the rehearsal ('tour'), but in the moments of actually getting there, the process, things are open-ended, unfixed, even impossibly haphazard. It is this unfixed, impossibly haphazard nature of processes of rehearsal that are of interest to me here. A performer/director/maker in rehearsal will find herself/himself regularly lacking panoptic knowledge of that performance, lacking an overview, or a view from above as a map might imply. Instead, s/he will often have a different knowledge of space: one that is about direction, movement, velocity and time, not one that is about an optical ordering. The map simply does not describe the experience of rehearsing. 'Touring' is a more appropriate metaphor to use in the study of the processes of rehearsing in contemporary devised performance, and simultaneously the study of the everyday processes of imagining our pasts, and, more importantly in terms of the subject matter of this edited collection, our futures.

Death is the one thing we can all be absolutely sure of and when we really encounter that real moment we say "it's like being in a film, or a play". The real is what you don't get most of the time. The real is those really traumatic things that happen to us, it's the basis of life. It's un-encounterable, but we do encounter it and when we do we tend to try to forget it or ignore it or we talk about it being as though it were happening to somebody else, or you're in a play or a film. Actual life is a kind of amalgam or weaving of what we call the symbolic and the imaginary so it's a weaving of the forms in which we communicate – speech, fashion, whatever. Plus how we imagine the world to be – God, poetry, making love, art, theatre, whatever – and the real is, in a way, this funny thing that's un-encounterable. But we do encounter it, but usually when we encounter it it's traumatic so we try to forget it, in other words the real is trauma. And the other one is it's like what art does often, like the movies and for most people that's their experience of art, for other people it might be "it's like that painting" but for most people it's like being in the movies … and in some senses art is able to articulate that aspect of ourselves that is beyond ourselves, what we might call the real, so when people say "it was just like the movies" they're trying to say "it's like my life but even more so". So, even though the real is not like the movies, and having been in a traumatic situation like being in a car crash or losing someone you love, is actually nothing like the movies, the reason why we use that as metaphor is that the movies are so much not like our lives, just like trauma is so much not like our lives.

(part of this story used by Martin in *Death Rattle*)

Playtext 1

The Rehearsal (a trilogy), Part 1: Death Rattle

CHARACTERS:

Peter and Martin (two men in their mid-sixties – Peter is slightly older. Martin is taller and slimmer than Peter and traditionally plays the straight man to Peter's comic).

SETTING:

Peter and Martin are sitting at different tables in a pub *with* the audience. Audience and performers are drinking beer.

SYNOPSIS:

Two sixty-something men towards the end of their double-act comedy career rehearse for an audition showreel for a radio show. Each reflects on the deaths of the people they have loved, the long endurance and hostility of their friendship, and their proximity to death.

CHOREOGRAPHY:

Throughout the show Peter and Martin rehearse five physical comedy routines. These physical choreographies are marked as 'Interludes' and need to be developed in rehearsal with the two performers.

Figure 1: Martin Buchan and Peter Kennedy in *Death Rattle*
(photo: Brian Slater).

AUDIENCE ROLE:

This is an interactive performance text where audience members are invited to act as sound effects operators in the rehearsal for and recording of a Radio 4 audition showreel. These audience members are on-script throughout and are 'rewarded' with extra beer.

PROPS:

Microphone and stand.

Two sound effects trays:

Sound effects tray 1: three party poppers, glass of water and straw, small door with handle that can open and close, charged electric drill, salad spinner.

Sound effects tray 2: aerosol can, egg and bowl, cabbage and knife, cat litter tray filled with cat litter (on floor), whistle, bucket with crockery.

Act 1: The Imagined

PETER: It's something that I talk about a lot actually and I know why I do it. It's because my father died when he was sixty-three and I've worked out why I do it. And I also do it coz I'm quite good at visualisation so um how do I do it? I imagine that I will die before I am sixty-five years old and the reason I do that is I'm the eldest son in my family and my father died before he was sixty-five years old. And my father, he was the eldest son in his family and his father died before he was sixty-five years old. In fact all of the males in my family have died before they reached sixty-five years old. So at some level I think I'm cursed, at another level I absolutely know that that isn't going to happen, but there's something about imagining it that makes the reality of it somehow not so bad. But then of course when I start thinking about it and I think oh no I really need to make some preparations and just having my stuff in order, making sure that everything will be arranged for my wife and for my children, well you can just get quite carried away with it, can't you?

MARTIN: I was in a show where all these people had to die on stage, and if you died in the last act it was fine but half way through the people were

33

struggling to stay awake, coz the people who died early were just lying there, and also if you stay motionless for long periods of time it's really difficult and they were really struggling with it, and this one guy would doze off every night and start to snore, and people were trying to kick him, it was a nightmare.

PETER: I remember once when I was doing a play and it was something that I was supposed to be very shocked about and it was not until almost the dress rehearsal, it was the run before the dress rehearsal and I was supposed to be looking at something and it was a really pornographic photograph that they gave me and they said that my look of shock was so funny but I could never reproduce that look again. They should have done it on the night, like that film, that one with Sigourney Weaver where the alien came out of John Hurt's chest and the actors didn't know about it and they were absolutely horrified. "I'm having these dark thoughts and I'm trying to protect you as much as I can but you need to be prepared for things coming your way". That's what my mother said. You know the French word for rehearsal is 'répétition', in Russian its 'repetitsiya', in Dutch 'repetitie' – repetition. Whereas in Italian its 'prova', Greek 'próva' and German 'probe', which is searching, seeking.

MARTIN: And I'm always told that you're never prepared, however much you go over and over it, it always takes you unawares, you'll see. Like when my mum died. I'd gone over it hundreds of times in my head, from when I was small, but I just wasn't prepared, it took me unawares. Even though I'd gone over it over and over again in my head. Repeating it.

PETER: But you'll only stop going over and over it when you pop your clogs.

MARTIN: I must have been thinking about my mother dying. She had Alzheimers and as a consequence she wasn't quite the person that we'd previously known and so when she died I'd kind of come to terms with it, even though I wasn't ready. She had always been very warm and generous. And as I got older the kind of things that became specific were the funeral. And we'd always have these slightly black but comic exchanges, where I'd ask, "what kind of music would you like to be played?"

PETER: "I wouldn't want it to be a sad ceremony, I'd want it to be happy".

MARTIN: Sometimes I look back and I feel I really didn't grieve very profoundly when she died but I think it was because I was ready for it, I can only assume that this was partly because I knew she was dying and I'd rehearsed it, so whatever was happening I wasn't close to her death as it happened, I'd anticipated it so that there was a lack of contact.

PETER: Like a rehearsed argument.

MARTIN: What's the point in having an argument for argument's sake? "We'll have none of that or we'll fight and argue with everybody". You are working towards an end for instance and you compromise – you have an argument with somebody demanding a hundred per cent but you have already set in your mind that you want to get fifty per cent. My wife she wanted a country house with the gardens, the hedges and ditches and everything else. We've got a town house with no hedges. It wasn't a compromise. But bedrooms – I'd worked out she wanted five, I wanted two, it came in at three.

PETER: Yes but you have to prepare the ground first. You have to dig the ground. I can taste the crop before I put it in that's why I put the beans in because of the flavour.

MARTIN: But if you don't do it now then you'll never do it. There are always really good reasons for not doing something, for not taking the plunge, um, but until you get into negotiations with those unknowns you never do it.

PETER: I don't live in the past or the future because you can't see into the future, you don't know what is going to come until you're dead. There's no God, no fate, nobody else knows anything about my future and I don't know about my future. I was called up to Malaysia, I didn't fancy going, I got out on health grounds, I got a perforated eardrum and they wouldn't accept me in the army. I was as chuffed as mint balls me. Malaysia ... Cyprus. I thought about what would happen all the time. I thought about not coming back. You know, you go over there you're going to get blown away. A lot of my mates got blown away. I was chuffed I didn't go. I'm still a bit deaf in one ear. A friend of mine, about 86, fought in the second world war. Tommy died a few years ago, he went out in '51.

MARTIN: My father died a few years ago. Before he died I asked what music he wanted played at his funeral and he was very quick, he came out and he said:

PETER: "That Bach piece 'Air on a G string'".

MARTIN: And I said is it anything to do with you smoking Hamlet cigars? We laughed. It was almost as if it took away that sense of grief. Instead it became a celebration. That was a very, very important acceptance of death for him and for me.

PETER: [*gets up to go to the bar*] Like when you rehearse things you don't often say, like I see people drop lots of litter and I think I'll go up and say something clever but often I chicken out because they'll be bigger than me or stronger and you rehearse it but you don't do it.

MARTIN: Like actors on stage playing people who are standing around in rehearsal. Pete, I want you to notice the way you are standing, notice the way your arms are. In real life everyone stands with their hands by their sides or having a conversation sitting with their legs crossed, with their hands touching their face. Don't stand facing the audience, it's not necessary. You can have your back to the audience. I think it is interesting to explore that.

PETER: I still quite like Stanislavski's idea of building up a back story, by which I mean you have a scene when they have to leave the little village, the little town where the three sisters live. It may be unfamiliar to the actor; this very understated Chekhovian text. They may need to generate stories in their performance that they'll never ever use but it gives them a kind of a background. Actors then feel as though they have more of a world. I generally find myself with a script in hand [*takes out his script, consults it, and reads out next couple of lines*]. Tommy said that after you'd been out there a long time you were more likely to act heroically, rather than if you'd only arrived yesterday, because you've become acquainted with death. It's your *acquaintance* with death that makes you accept it rather like you accept a friend doing something wrong rather than a stranger.

MARTIN: Death is the one thing we can all be absolutely sure of and when we really encounter that real moment we say "it's like being in a film, or a play". The real is what you don't get most of the time. The real is those really traumatic things that happen to us, it's the basis of life. It's un-encounterable, but we do encounter it and when we do we tend to forget it or ignore it or we talk about it being as though it were happening to somebody else, or you're in a play or a film. And it's different from how we *imagine* the world to be – God, poetry, making love, whatever. You have an accident and you lose your memory. That is one of the manifestations of the real, in other words the real is trauma, and trauma is so much not part of our everyday lives so we say it's like in the movies. If I tore open your stomach and pulled out your intestines you might say that's *real* life. I put my hand in your heart and pull your heart out, you might say that's the *real* me. And it's different from how I imagine it, to God, poetry, making love, whatever.

PETER: But without your heart and your lungs you wouldn't exist. And God doesn't exist.

MARTIN: So Pete, when you die and go to heaven, what will you say when you do come face-to-face with God?

PETER: I shall say "God. God. Why did you make the evidence of your existence so insubstantial?"

MARTIN: Isn't that what Bertrand Russell is supposed to have said?

PETER: Yeah. Good, isn't it?

BOTH: [*Improvised: Tell us about your stories – Have you ever imagined dying? – Have you imagined the people you love dying? – The actors should revisit, or refer to, the stories told here whenever they can throughout the rest of the show.*]

MARTIN: Ladies and Gentlemen, I'd just like to interrupt at this moment if I may, because it's Peter's birthday tomorrow, sixty-five … [*Assistants bring birthday cake lighted with sixty-five candles on it to Peter as all sing Happy Birthday. Peter blows out candles and plays 'embarrassed'*].

INTERLUDE 1: *Simultaneously Peter and Martin perform their interludes 2 (p 40) and 4 (p 51). They are performed as 'naturally' as possible (not comically).*

Act 2: Setting the Scene

BOTH: [*Improvised: Welcome – "I'm Peter/Martin" – A toast – We're here today to rehearse and record a showreel for Radio 4 – They're doing a new series on death and dying and are looking for two new presenters – We thought a comedy double-act might be quite original, and we are getting on a bit! Getting closer to death! We thought it might be an angle for them! – A kind of audition for them (our last chance etc.) – It's a routine about death, about dying, about getting ready for death, preparing for it – Our agents are here tonight, I'd like to introduce them (introduce members of audience as agents; Peter's agent is called Shelley) – Also our sound effects operator didn't turn up so we need two volunteers to operate sound effects (find volunteers and give them highlighted scripts (SOUND EFFECTS OPERATORS 1 and 2) and sound effects trays).*]

PETER: Don't worry there's no lines for you to say.

MARTIN: Just a thought about lines, I had a really bad experience in one show …

PETER: We'd better get a Prompt then. [*Gives a member of audience Prompt script and points out their place in it*] Can you prompt him if he forgets his lines?

PROMPT: Yes OK.

PETER: If he forgets his lines or maybe [*clicks*] can you give him his line?

PROMPT: Yes OK.

MARTIN: Are you sure you want her/him?

PETER: Yes. Why? Do you want another one? Do you want two? You *can* get quite bad and you do have a long speech now.

MARTIN: No I don't want two thanks, just wondering about her/him. I had a really bad experience in one show, it's about the way I learn lines, I tend to learn slowly but I will get there, do you know what I mean? Anyway it ended up that some people were off book in about a week and I wasn't and it just caused issues and we actually got into, well it got quite intense actually. We were rehearsing this piece and we only had two weeks to rehearse and it was a full Ayckbourn play to rehearse in two weeks and the information that I didn't get was that we were supposed to be off book before we got there and I didn't get that information and I arrived and they'd already learnt it. And I can't learn lines like that any way, so I arrived thinking "oh it's the usual, a read-through", and that was it really, from then on I was playing catch-up. But by the end of week one we'd kind of blocked it and they were off book completely and I still had the book in my hand. I had the *gist* of it, and by week two I was fine but it got to the point where I'd try to put the script down and then try and get props and that just made it worse. It got to the point where if there was a prompt there'd be a silence and they'd all be like (humph) … [*clicks*]

PROMPT: And you can't work like that.

MARTIN: And you can't work like that …

PETER: [*to Prompt*] What's his next line?

PROMPT: I don't fucking want to work with you.

PETER: [*to Prompt – annoyed*] I don't want to fucking work with you.

MARTIN: I told you we should have got someone else … "I don't fucking want to work with you" I thought on the Saturday. I was trying without the script and it got to the third prompt and the director just exploded and I thought "I don't want to fucking work with you. I don't want to get in a row". And I nearly walked out, I've never walked out of a show, but I was that close, I just went out for an hour and calmed down.

PETER: [*indicates Prompt's script*] The thing to remember is we will always have a script on stage. We can keep it on the right page. But you've also got a Prompt to be on the safe side. [*to Prompt*]You'd better watch this bit coz he's not usually very good at it …

INTERLUDE 2: *During the above, Peter walks to the bar and indicates to Prompt asking whether s/he would like another beer, indicates three beers to the bartender, drops a ten pound note on the floor, bends unsteadily to pick it up, then begins to pay the bartender. Before he can pay, Martin asks him to repeat this section (and tiny details within it) directing him with the following words (we realise that Peter's action is very specific, detailed and exactly repeatable, and the routine gets increasingly funny):*

MARTIN: Yeah and then I'll clap you, OK again, again, again, OK again, again, if you come down like that and point to this person yeah? Show me yes. Yes! You have to point to the same person every time, it would be better, step ahaa to the bar and step to the bar. Yes, that's it! And step, ahaa, step. Again. Again. AGAIN. Do it fast yeah, so that … OK that's fine, that's fine, let's do that. Lets do the first again, again, the first bit, it will make all the difference. Lovely. That's great. All those points, that's good that's like a bolero. On the second one wait until you truly get down and then you can sway a little. Right, so sway. Can we try that one again? Let's do it quite small, that might be nice actually, yes so that it's quite gradual, that one. So it's quite safe. How does that feel? Is it strong?

PETER: It's strong.

MARTIN: Does it feel safe?

PETER: It feels safe.

MARTIN: Is it alright?

PETER: It's alright.

MARTIN: That's good. Can you just do that one once more, from the other direction? How does that feel? I'm not sure about it from the other direction. You have to indicate it again first and then I'll come in. And then start and go. [*Peter manages finally to pay the bartender, and give one beer to the Prompt*] Looking good Pete. Looking good.

[*They go to the bar and drink the two beers at the bar.*]

PETER: My landlady's taken the bloody door off, she said that she'd taken the door off to repair it and took off the panel and it's a bottom panel so I reckon it's been kicked in.

MARTIN: Where is the door?

PETER: It's propped up in the room.

MARTIN: It's just not on?

PETER: It's just not on.

MARTIN: Can you put the door in the hole?

PETER: That's what happens tonight, the door is going in the hole.

MARTIN: Have you got some other contacts for him Shelley? [*Peter's agent – indicate the audience member from earlier*] It doesn't sound too good, does it?

PETER: No it doesn't sound too good.

MARTIN: If all else fails you can always kip down at mine.

PETER: The thing is that I can park up there and walk here.

MARTIN: You can do that at mine. She might have put the door on by the time you get home.

PETER: Well the house is lovely and clean.

MARTIN: She can't expect you not to have a door. Shelley will get you some more contacts in case?

PETER: We'll see how it goes tonight.

SOUND EFFECTS OPERATOR 2:   [*Stand up and take five slow steps through cat litter.*]

MARTIN: OK so let's think about the showreel. It's got to sound good. Like they're enjoying themselves. Like we're actually good. Like they're

41

actually enjoying being here. Listening to us. Let's get the audience involved somehow. What can we get them to do? [*adlib*]

PETER: If you're going to make new lines up, I can do that …

PETER: Applause and laughter, give them some training in that …

MARTIN: Isn't that my line?

PETER: No it's my line Martin.

MARTIN: [*to Prompt*] So what's my line?

PROMPT: Being cued in.

MARTIN: Yes I know I'm being cued in, but what's my line?

PROMPT: Being cued in.

MARTIN: Oh … being cued in.

PETER: Try laughing, laughter boards.

MARTIN: Holding up signs.

PETER: [*checks microphone etc.*] Dying, it's not normal sort of stuff, so we'd have to get them mourning and crying. Their facial expressions. Is that a convincing mourning face and if it's not then?

MARTIN: We'd better just run through the health and safety issues. I'll just have to run through the health and safety issues with the audience and the sound effects operators. [*adlib*]

PETER: [*on microphone*] Has anyone lost anyone recently? Perhaps you could show us the right face, stand up and show us. [*adlib*]

MARTIN: Have you been in touch since? Peter Kaye did something and it was quite dark, "have you had your liver checked?" For the sake of entertainment. It got really dark, "I think you're really ill".

PETER: That song as well.

MARTIN: A singalong dirge.

PETER: Latin. Let's have a break and have a song.

MARTIN: Some sort of noise they can make.

PETER: A death rattle.

MARTIN: If you think the comic's bombing give him the death rattle.

SOUND EFFECTS OPERATOR 1:   [*Open door and close with bang.*]

MARTIN: How about a pub quiz, or an ongoing quiz? 10 questions as you go through the show, songs about death …

PETER: Longest screen death, murderers …

MARTIN: You could recreate screen deaths – John Wayne's …

[*Peter and Martin re-enact a Western shoot-out.*]

SOUND EFFECTS OPERATOR 1:   [*Pull party popper 1 when Peter shoots Martin.* Martin dies theatrically. *Pull party popper 2 when Peter points his gun to the floor.* Peter jumps and looks at gun. *Pull party popper 3 when Peter looks at his gun.* Peter dies theatrically.]

MARTIN: Crippin.

PETER: Christie.

MARTIN: John Hurt.

PETER: My son played him, terrible.

MARTIN: 10 Rillington Place.

PETER: Did he poison them?

MARTIN: No he gassed them.

SOUNDS EFFECTS OPERATOR 2:   [*short spray of aerosol*]

PETER: He gassed them [*spray*], gassed them [*spray*] and strangled them …
                 I'll bring my son in, he could do it really convincingly.

MARTIN: That guy in London who shoved them down the drains and they
                 found that there was a murderer coz all the drains were blocked …

SOUND EFFECTS OPERATOR 1:   [*assistant has brought microphone to SOUND
                 EFFECTS OPERATOR 1. Blow through straw into glass of water to
                 make bubbling sound. On microphone.*]

PETER: Nielson.

MARTIN: … and he was picking up blokes in a pub, taking them back, killing
                 them …

SOUND EFFECTS OPERATOR 1:   [*Drill for three seconds. On microphone.*]

SOUND EFFECTS OPERATOR 2:   [*Drop an egg into bowl. On microphone.*]

SOUND EFFECTS OPERATOR 1:   [*Spin salad spinner for three seconds. On
                 microphone.*]

MARTIN: … chopping them up …

SOUND EFFECTS OPERATOR 2:   [*Cut cabbage in half with knife. On microphone.*]

MARTIN: … and putting them down the drains.

SOUND EFFECTS OPERATOR 1:   [*Blow through straw into glass of water. On
                 microphone.*]

PETER: "It's about time you went" and that would signify that he was about
                 to murder them. "It's about time you went" [*Scottish accent*].

SOUND EFFECTS OPERATOR 1:   [*Open door and close with bang.*]

SOUND EFFECTS OPERATOR 2:   [*Stand up and take five slow steps through cat litter.*]

MARTIN: That's great – you're really good at that – great timing. What do you think Shelley? [*adlib*] Show, let's think about the shows that we've heard recently that we really like …

PETER: Yeah.

MARTIN: … that might be usable, re-usable. Show-wise.

PETER: Well I saw Spike Milligan once. In a real plush theatre. You know, a proper theatre, none of this site-specific nonsense – a proper theatre with plush red curtains – in London somewhere. The audience loved him. Mind you it was a student audience. Students love anything. But he got to the end and he took a bow and they applauded and were shouting "more, more". He came back on, told another joke and then bowed again. And they applauded again, even louder, and he came back and took another bow, and said "I've got to go now, I've got a train to catch". And they wouldn't let him go, and he came back on again and he said "I've got to go – now Fuck Off", and they all laughed again and applauded, and he came back again and said "Fuck Off", and this had them in stitches, and he came back again and he said [*screaming desperately*] "FUCK OFF. FUCK OFF. FUCK OFF."

MARTIN: Was this real? That really happened?

PETER: Yeah yeah.

MARTIN: Wow.

PETER: We probably couldn't do that though.

MARTIN: No.

PETER: It was a really good show.

MARTIN: It sounds it.

MARTIN: Well I saw this production of some British farce or other – a play within a play, a play about the putting on of a play. The first act is the dress rehearsal with lots of exits and entrances, missed cues, crap props – something about sardines. The second act is the performance itself, but this time everything's switched round and it's backstage, and we see them all falling out, and the show is rubbish and we see them running on and off stage, and things going wrong, and loads of slapstick. And they keep running off from one door and in through a totally different door and they're obviously knackered, all these old guys running frantically on and off stage! So I'm Martin, and Pete, you're Peter. OK so your line will be "Is that the front door?" OK? ['*acting*'] "I'll just go and see what's happening" [*exits 'stage-left'*].

PETER: [*to audience*] Not much of a line, is it? ['*acting*'] "Is that the front door?" [*pause*] "Is that the front door?" [*long awkward pause*] "I thought I heard the front door".

SOUND EFFECTS OPERATOR 1: [*Open door slowly and close door with bang.*]

SOUND EFFECTS OPERATOR 2: [*Stand up and take five quick steps through cat litter.*]

MARTIN: [*enters 'stage right' – has had to run a longish way to get from one bar exit to another and is panting*]. Fuck me … That kind of stuff … kills me …

PETER: Was this real? That really happened?

MARTIN: No not really Pete, it was a play.

PETER: Wow.

MARTIN: I don't want to do that though, too physical for me …

PETER: I quite enjoyed it actually.

MARTIN: It was a really good show.

PETER: It sounds it. Have you got that? Let's fix it on paper.

[*both write notes in notebooks*]

MARTIN: Why, when you write your rehearsal notes, they're always diagrammatical, aren't they? Literally more so, I don't know, I think more so than mine.

PETER: Yeah.

MARTIN: Yeah, I used to do it, I think it's more about journeys for you, I used to do it but now I can't understand the diagrams.

PETER: If I know the general direction, I can then … piece together the other bits. If you had written, if you had written down the curve you're supposed to do when you enter in a diagrammatical way then you, then you would have remembered it.

MARTIN: The curve? What, when I cross the stage after I enter? You think so? I just don't get them. The diagrams. I think I can only really try and commit it to memory because going over the diagrams I found I had to keep going back to the place I'd been to because there was so many times going back to the same point that there was no way to differentiate what was where. I think that's why I've always preferred radio, I don't have to remember where I'm standing or where I'm walking or what curve I'm taking when I enter.

PETER: [*using his diagram in the notebook begins to demonstrate*] I'd have loved to have done more theatre in my time. I think it would have suited me, all the rehearsals, all the repetition, all the details. See, what you do is you navigate your way as though it were a map – you place yourself inside the diagram and you move with it. [*improvised: See here is the curve etc. …*]

INTERLUDE 3: *Peter 'glides' around the stage (as Bach's "Air on a G String" gradually becomes louder and louder) – he is following the diagrams drawn in his notebook to demonstrate to Martin the 'curve'.*

Act 3: Endings

MARTIN: Beautiful Pete, but rather redundant as we're doing radio. Ladies and Gentlemen, I'd just like to interrupt at this moment if I may, because it's Peter's birthday tomorrow, sixty-five … [*assistants bring birthday cake lighted with sixty-five candles on it to Pete as all sing Happy Birthday. Pete blows out candles and plays slightly more 'embarrassed'*].

MARTIN: Now, let's think about the ending of the showreel. We're having problems deciding on an ending so we probably need your help.

PETER: We've got two options. Perhaps we'll show you them and you can decide. So option one:

MARTIN: I'll introduce you.

PETER: I don't think I need any introduction.

Option 1:

[*Peter and Martin sit at a table on which rests a large set of Victorian-style weighing scales. Each has a cup of tea and a pile of pebbles on the table in front of him. Peter has a small pile of pebbles. Martin has a larger pile. After each actor speaks his line, he tosses a pebble onto his side of the scales. At the opening, the scales are heavily weighted towards Peter – when all pebbles have been placed on the scales in this way, the last pebble should tip the scales in Martin's favour. Both are on microphone.*]

PETER: We're nearly there, mate. At the pivotal moment.

MARTIN: How so?

PETER: They worked it out, didn't you hear? The scientists, the boffins. They worked out that there'll soon be more of us than there are of them.

MARTIN: Oh, right. What?

PETER: Us, the living. Them, the dead. Any moment now, there'll be more living people than dead people. You should be honoured. This is a pivotal moment in history you're witnessing.

MARTIN: Are you sure? This sounds like one of those urban myths to me. How can they know how many there are?

PETER: They have their means. Satellites, questionnaires, door-to-door … prying.

MARTIN: I mean how many dead?

PETER: Oh, they do excavations. They rummage through libraries, work out all the begetting. And of course when someone goes from our side, they're automatically chalked up to the other side. It's modelled on computers.

MARTIN: Blimey. The things they get grants for [*makes to toss a pebble on scales, then pauses*]. But hang on – all those dead people in prehistoric times, and biblical times, and medieval times. There must be loads. And I mean malaria, HIV. All the wars. There must be thousands of people dying, right now. It just doesn't seem plausible.

PETER: You're underestimating how much fucking goes on.

MARTIN: I suppose so.

PETER: All over the world, right now, people are at it. And it's increasing, the fucking, year on year. There's more than ever before. I mean, imagine how many people are coming in China right now, as I speak.

[*Martin and Peter share a moment of quiet contemplation, eyes closed.*]

PETER: You watch the news and it's just about the stuff that kills you. But that's just half the story. The other side is people having sex and babies being born. That's the news.

MARTIN: [*peers at Peter's pile of pebbles*] Your pile's running a bit low. Do you need some more?

PETER: You're only allowed a set amount. It's the rules.

MARTIN: Give over. That's a myth.

PETER: It's true. From tiny insects to giant tortoises. They just get through them at different rates.

MARTIN: I'm pretty sure that's not true. [*still looking at Peter's pile, with only a handful of pebbles left*] You could be the one, you know, to tip the scales for the dead. That would be something, wouldn't it? A consolation.

PETER: Huh.

MARTIN: More than a consolation. You'd go down in history.

PETER: No one would notice, probably.

MARTIN: Just imagine – out of all the millions of people. It'd be like winning the lottery. It could be you.

PETER: Or it could be someone else, right now, on the other side of the world.

MARTIN: But it could be you.

PETER: I'm not sure I care that much.

[*Peter tosses last pebble.*]

MARTIN: Well, in some ways I envy you.

[*Peter very slowly slumps forward until his forehead rests on the table. He drops crockery and at the same time …*]

SOUND EFFECTS OPERATOR 2:   [*Drop crockery into bucket.*]

[*Martin's hand, holding a pebble, hovers over the scales. He looks at Peter.*]

MARTIN: Pete? Pete? [*He shakes Pete gently. A long pause.*] You're not dead, are you? [*he scrutinises the scales*] It was asking a bit much [*drops pebble onto scales*] that we would get it right [*pebble*]. First time [*pebble*]. I mean what were the chances [*pebble*] really [*pebble*]? It [*pebble*] comes [*pebble*] with [*pebble*] practice [*pebble*], with [*pebble*] trial [*pebble*] and [*pebble*] error [*pebble*]. And [*pebble*] they [*pebble*] don't [*pebble*] let [*pebble*] you [*pebble*] rehearse [*pebble*] there's [*pebble*] not [*pebble*] enough [*pebble*] time [*pebble*] to [*pebble*] rehearse. [*Martin drops his last pebble onto the scales then slowly slumps onto the table beside Pete. He drops crockery.*]

SOUND EFFECTS OPERATOR 2:   [*Drop crockery into bucket.*]

BOTH: And that's option number one. Keep it in mind [*adlib*]. And here is option number two:

Option 2:

INTERLUDE 4: *Martin begins to talk with a woman, asking if she wants a drink and getting her a drink from the bar, moving between her and the bar, he is chatting her up. Pete watches for a while then asks him to repeat this as he directs him with following (we realise that Martin's action is very specific, detailed and exactly repeatable, and the routine gets increasingly funny):*

PETER: Let's try again. Go into the left first, turn towards her left and turn right, not away from her, that's it. So that way and go there, do that again. I like that change, that step, that's right, turn right, yes, change it slightly, go back, right ahaa. Will we practice you going out? We need to get a bit closer, that's right, is that going to be OK? That's impressive, just try again. Breathless, this one will be the last time you need to reach out. You don't need to do that until the second time, let's go back, where are you before you go over here? Are you over here? Can you? Do it round here, at the bar. You know where you need to be, just the once, yeah brilliant [*the routine starts to get a little more energetic*]. Really good, that was the right time to do that, no it's actually the first time, that's the second step. Balance and lean, bring it out, then lean. Great, that's lovely, can we just go back a bit, the spin, can you bring her back in and lean, that's good. Yes. And throw him off [*to the audience member*]. And run that way [*to Martin*].

[*Martin runs out of the same exit as he used the last time*]

PETER: Am I going too far?

INTERLUDE 5: *Martin, after his exit runs round to the other entrance and enters. Peter orders Martin to run round three more times and when Martin is off, Peter adlibs with audience, talks about the actor having to adlib and fill awkward pauses etc. On fourth exit, Martin fails to return. Peter goes out to find him and comes back in very worried.*

PETER: I've never seen him like that before. Is there anyone here with any medical knowledge?

[*Martin re-enters.*]

BOTH: And that's option number two. Let's take a vote. [*the audience vote*]

Act 4: The Argument

MARTIN: OK, so that's the endings, let's think about some beginnings and middles, any ideas, scenarios?

PETER: I was thinking of a failed comedy duo.

MARTIN: Oh yes.

PETER: And that could be … they could really get at each other.

MARTIN: And never get the lines right.

PETER: Funny that, coz you're actually pretty good at learning lines …

PETER: Been together a long time.

MARTIN: Quite bitter.

PETER: There was a film made, Walter Matthau.

MARTIN: *The Sunshine Boys*?

PETER: Yes. His daughter gets them to meet after a long time.

MARTIN: Yeah, but they're geriatrics, aren't they?

PETER: Cannon and Ball have got back together if that's any inspiration.

MARTIN: There's a dependency overall between the actors, I like the idea.

PETER: There's a discrepancy of shape, isn't there? And that makes me laugh straight away.

MARTIN: Little and Large. You don't need lines for that. I could say, aren't you growing a bit? There's no gags in that, stop growing or …

PETER: So I'm the butt then? I'm the butt of the jokes. Alright. I could worry about you and you could get really pissed off with me worrying about you.

MARTIN: I like that, it's really honest.

PETER: And you could make me worry even more.

MARTIN: And if you incorporate the lines into it, you could be worried that I'm going to lose my lines and then you lose them and that makes you worry even more. "I've never got that line wrong in my life".

PETER: The thing to remember is you will always have a script on stage. But in this kind of work there's very little certainty until you go on stage. If there *is* a stage. You have to recognise that it's not built in stone and it can move, so it's no good having a go at each other about the lines because the lines have only formed hours before you're up there. So you learn the lines but on the night it's bound to be different because the audience are there and they're a little close.

MARTIN: But the lines have to be exactly the same.

PETER: That would cease to be funny.

MARTIN: Ladies and Gentlemen, I'd just like to interrupt at this moment if I may, because it's Peter's birthday tomorrow, sixty-five … [*assistants bring birthday cake lighted with sixty-five candles on it to Peter as all sing Happy Birthday. Peter blows out candles and plays even more 'embarrassed'*].

SOUND EFFECTS OPERATOR 2: [*After "Happy Birthday" has been sung, blow whistle.*]

MARTIN: How's that for sound levels?

TECHNICAL OPERATOR: Great, thanks Martin.

MARTIN: I like the idea that the audience are at a recording. It could be recorded for radio, with a sound effects tray.

PETER: I saw this radio recording and there was a door being used as a sound effect and it was a tiny door that opened and shut onto the floor, but the woman operating it was always late.

SOUND EFFECTS OPERATOR 1:   [*Pause for five seconds then open door quickly and close with bang.*]

MARTIN: So we deliberately give them the wrong cues so that they come in late or in completely the wrong place.

PETER: I love the idea of dropping crockery …

SOUND EFFECTS OPERATOR 2:   [*Drop crockery into bucket.*]

PETER: and canned applause …

[*canned applause*]

PETER: and laughter.

[*canned laughter*]

MARTIN: So at the beginning we preface the show by saying that this is something that we're trying to sell to Radio 4, this is a demo tape, and we need your help to make it successful.

PETER: And our careers are really hinging on it, and there are producers in the audience here tonight.

MARTIN: We can even point someone out – our agents. [*adlib*]

INTERLUDE 6: *Martin moves through the bar to indicate the agents – it's a simple walk but with a specific detail (e.g. hitching trousers up at specific moment, a comedy trip), and is vaguely 'curved'. Peter begins to direct Martin.*

PETER: Repeat [*Martin repeats his walk*]. Repeat. Repeat. Repeat.

MARTIN: Alright I know it now.

PETER: For Christ's sake, I know I am a perfectionist, I'll admit that.

MARTIN: I can't work like this. It's not helpful, is it? I mean we have to work together anyway, so it's pointless being bloody-minded like that. You keep picking me up on things that I'm fine with and it really bugs me …

PETER: You missed the bloody curve, didn't you?

MARTIN: Well so you say, so you say, but I bloody well got it in my head. I knew exactly what to do next …

PETER: No no no no.

MARTIN: Just listen a minute, will you? The fact was I bloody knew what I was going to do and if you'd just waited … but you can never bloody wait.

PETER: There was no curve, alright? No curve.

MARTIN: Is that important?

PETER: It is important, that's why I kept doing it again and again and again, to see if you could find the curve but you never did. All this stuff up here was OK. And you've got the gist of your lines …

MARTIN: Yeah thank you, thank you.

PETER: Right it was fine but the base …

MARTIN: Fine, fine.

PETER: The base, the base.

MARTIN: Yeah?

PETER: You didn't get the curve.

MARTIN: I don't give a damn about the curve.

PETER: Exactly, you'd settle for anything, wouldn't you … the gist of the lines.

MARTIN: Will you listen to me? Because the audience aren't going to see the curve. They're not going to notice the bloody curve, just coz you've got it in your head that there's a curve.

PETER: Well, you are a twat.

MARTIN: Oh yes go on abuse me …

PETER: I use technical language. I've got the diagrams somewhere … I talk about the curve, you talk about it as if it doesn't exist and it doesn't matter, well the curve does matter and the people will notice. And they'll also notice if you don't catch up with me on the lines.

MARTIN: This is bloody typical, typical. And we can never make any sense of those diagrams anyway. I don't like being told by you what to do, I know damn well what to do, I've been doing it as long as you have. Well nearly as long anyway.

PETER: Exactly. Nearly as long.

MARTIN: Well yeah …

PETER: Well I come from a different time, don't I? And perhaps that's what the problem is. Everybody knew about curves in my time.

MARTIN: It's not a bloody musical here, it's not bloody variety.

PETER: In my time you didn't need to tell people there was a curve. I get letters about my curves.

MARTIN: Oh yeah, and exactly how many BAFTAs have you got then?

PETER: You're not funny. You've ceased to be funny.

MARTIN: And you are? I'm supposed to be the straight man and you're the bloody funny one, you get the laughs, all the payoff, I don't get that, I just set you up all the time.

PETER: Except when I'm the butt, when there's anything to do with height, fatness. I'm the butt, aren't I? Anything like that and you start getting the laughs and they are not your laughs. They are not your laughs.

MARTIN: Why do I do that? Because they are bloody good visual gags, because the audience can see it. It's obvious, we don't have to do anything, we don't have to work at that, they can bloody see it.

PETER: And that's about the limit of your imagination, isn't it? Things that you don't have to work at, like the curve. And the lines.

MARTIN: Shut up about the fucking curve. That's a really small thing … and the lines was a one off …

PETER: Small! There you go, you gotta get that in, haven't you?

MARTIN: You're always picking me up on bloody little details …

PETER: Little!

MARTIN: Don't be stupid Peter, I'm not playing your stupid games.

PETER: Oh yes, I know I haven't quite got your *towering* talent.

MARTIN: I want to get this right, I want to do it properly.

PETER: You're just *bearing down* on me …

MARTIN: That's *your* problem.

PETER: *My* problem is the curve. You haven't got it. You haven't got the basic fundamental curve.

MARTIN: And your prompt line, it isn't funny, I know my lines, you don't need to tell me. You think that's funny, don't you? You think because I had a problem once that it's funny.

PETER: Yeah, I do think that's funny actually.

MARTIN: Do you?

PETER: Yeah I do.

MARTIN: Well it isn't bloody funny to me, I'll tell you it isn't bloody funny at all.

PETER: Oh fuck off.

MARTIN: No you fuck off.

PETER: [*screaming desperately as in Spike Milligan story earlier*] FUCK OFF. FUCK OFF. FUCK OFF.

[*pause*]

MARTIN: Can you do that again with a curve?

PETER: For God's sake. Let's do this fucking stupid recording. It's you that wants to be on Radio 4, not me, with all those God-Botherers on Thought for the Day. I don't want to be on Radio 4. It's not really me. And I don't want to talk about death and dying. There's nothing to be said about it. I'm going to die and that's it. Nothing. Nothing. No God. No judgement. Nobody is planning my death up there. So I'm not going to plan it down here.

MARTIN: So Pete, what would you say if you died and you *did* come face-to-face with God?

PETER: I would say "God. God. Why did you make the evidence of your existence so insubstantial?"

MARTIN: Isn't that what Bertrand Russell is supposed to have said?

PETER: Yeah. Good isn't it?

MARTIN: That's all OK Pete, but I think it needs a bit of background music [*to technical operator*], what have we got?

[*Technical operator plays sequence of music from a fantasy funeral playlist e.g. Bette Midler's "The Rose", Elton John's "Candle in the Wind", Robbie Williams's "Angels". Peter refuses all of these and they finally settle on Bach's "Air on a G String".*]

MARTIN: OK, are we all ready for a recording? Lets do it. [*adlib*]

Act 5: Playing Dead (Radio showreel)

[*on microphones with Bach playing*]

MARTIN: We get used to the idea of our own deaths as we get older I think because more and more people we know die. If you're surrounded by people dying you have a premature acceptance of death and religion tries to prepare you for death.

PETER: That's why I think religion is a selfish thing because it's just there to make you feel better, that you're going to reunite with everyone that you love. It's a comfort for them too.

MARTIN: But it is quite hard accepting that you are never going to see them again. Every morning I look in the mirror and I think I'm not going to see her again, I'm not going to see her again. OK, so how do I get through the day knowing that? How do I manage that knowledge? I've no idea what the etymology of rehearsing is but it's not just about repetition, it's about searching or seeking, it must be about looking to the future. You do that when you get up in the morning and look in the mirror and think "how am I going to look today?" "What kind of trousers shall I wear?" "What kind of dress shall I wear?" It's all a rehearsal for something. In a sense you never live in the present, you always live in some kind of idea of the future or trapped by some memory of the past so it's all a rehearsal in that sense.

PETER: We could do with some humorous stories, jokes, or antidotes to liven things up a bit.

MARTIN: I was sorry to hear that your buried your father.

PETER: Well, we had to, you know, he was dead.

MARTIN: Peter once thought that he was dead. We took him to a psychiatrist who couldn't seem to get through to him and get him to believe that he was still alive. So the psychiatrist took a different approach and showed him loads of medical books that demonstrated that dead men don't bleed. Eventually Peter seemed convinced that dead men don't bleed. "Do you now agree that dead men don't bleed?"

PETER: "Yes, I do."

MARTIN: "Very well then" the psychiatrist said and he took out a pin and pricked Peter's finger. Out came a trickle of blood."What does that tell you Peter?"

Figure 2: Peter Kennedy with Louise Bennett in *Death Rattle* (photo: Brian Slater).

PETER: "Oh my god … Dead men *do* bleed." I live every day like it's my last. Every morning I wake up early and spend three hours on the phone making funeral arrangements. I imagine myself dying heroically. I'm going to die anyway, so why not die heroically? Like what the First World War heroes must have thought. I'm going to die anyway, so why not die heroically? And when I die I want to be dressed in my best suit so that my friends can see the body of a dead atheist and say "There he is. All dressed up and no place to go."

MARTIN: So Pete, what will you say when you die and you come face-to-face with God?

PETER: I shall say "God. God. Why did you make the evidence of your existence so insubstantial?" Mother Teresa died and went to heaven. She was greeted at the Pearly Gates by God who asked if she was hungry. She said that she was. So God opened a can of baked beans and made some toast. While she ate her beans on toast Mother Teresa looked down into hell and saw the inhabitants devouring steak and chips, lobster thermidore, caviar and pannacotta. Curious, but deeply trusting, she remained quiet. The next day God again asked Mother Teresa to join him for dinner. Again it was beans on toast. Again, Mother Teresa could see the inhabitants of Hell enjoying Beef Wellington, moules mariniere, chicken tikka masala and bread and butter pudding. Still she said nothing. The following day, God made Mother Teresa beans on toast again. She couldn't take it any longer. Meekly, she asked:

MARTIN: "God I am grateful to be in heaven with you as a reward for the pious, obedient life I led. But here in heaven all I get to eat is beans on toast and in the Other Place they eat like emperors and kings. I just don't understand it …".

PETER: God sighed "Let's be honest Teresa, for just two people, it doesn't pay to cook".

MARTIN: I am much possessed by death. In imagining my own death I ask myself what would I want from others? Imagining the death of someone I love is not hard to do. Many of us here already are, in a sense, at the age of grief, where we've lost someone. My wife died three weeks ago.

PETER: Did she say anything before she died?

MARTIN: She spoke without interruption for about forty years.

PETER: I imagine myself not being here, and I imagine other people imagining me dead.

MARTIN: I have an ongoing conversation with my wife. She is there as some kind of ghost presence. To see my wife dead was very hard. She did not look good. These conversations make a difference for me. And they change my relation to the past, my memories of the past, what the meanings of my own history have for me. And those changes affect the way I'm behaving in the present.

PETER: Allow yourself to imagine that you are dead. Let it sink in. Realise that you no long exist as a living, breathing presence for anyone. Not your wife, not you children or grandchildren. Not your old friends or recent acquaintances. The only things left are your belongings, your script and whatever memories people carry with them. We never get any direction for it. We never get any feedback.

Act 6: Endings

[*Depends on what audience voted for earlier. Each ending is a recording played over sound system, with "Air on a G String" gradually swelling to the end.*]

Ending 1:

[*Crockery drops.*]

MARTIN: Pete? Pete? [*A long pause*] You're not dead, are you? It was asking a bit much [*drops pebble onto scales*] that we would get it right [*pebble*]. First time [*pebble*]. I mean what were the chances [*pebble*] really [*pebble*]? It [*pebble*] comes [*pebble*] with [*pebble*] practice [*pebble*], with [*pebble*] trial [*pebble*] and [*pebble*] error [*pebble*]. And [*pebble*] they [*pebble*] don't [*pebble*] let [*pebble*] you [*pebble*] rehearse [*pebble*] there's [*pebble*] not [*pebble*] enough [*pebble*] time [*pebble*] to [*pebble*] rehearse.

[*Crockery drops.*]

Ending 2:

MARTIN: [*Breathes heavily as though running in and out of bar with sound effects of door opening and closing and running through cat litter.*]

[*silence*]

PETER: Martin, Martin?

[*Sound effect of Peter exiting to look for Martin and coming back in quickly (door and cat litter).*]

PETER: I've never seen him like this before. Is there anyone here with any medical knowledge?

THE END

Chapter 2

I'm Dead, You're Dead: Imagining and Rehearsing (for) The End

Allan Kellehear

In the Melanesian islands of New Hebrides, a young man must undergo a remarkable test to ascertain whether he is worthy of life. This rite of passage imitates the path of the soul on its final journey to the land of the dead. The symbolic rite initiates the young man into life.

The initiate walks to a cave. At the entrance, the symbolic meeting place of life and death, a devouring female ghost sits blocking his way. Her name is Le-Hev-Hev. With her finger, this monster draws a geometric figure in the sand and waits patiently to be approached. At first, the sight of her makes the man confused by his own fear. But he regains his senses and moves towards her. As he does so, Le-Hev-Hev rubs out half of the design. Now the initiate, who is also known as the 'dead man', must redraw the figure or be destroyed by Le-Hev-Hev....

Now the question is: can he redraw it? There are several clues that readers or listeners of this story need before they can answer. The initiate needs to see how much of the pattern remains. This pattern will be complex, but the complexity is good. The patterns that remain are his past life. And they are there because Le-Hev-Hev cannot erase them. Your past life experiences and meanings are irrevocably yours. Only possibilities can be tampered with.

In a way, the missing pattern in the sand might be extended and re-drawn by attempting to make it mirror or reflect the existing pattern. Many attempt to draw their future in this way, especially those who are happy with their past life. But the missing pattern might be re-drawn differently from the one on the other side, especially by those wishing to forge a new life pattern. But readers and listeners should ask themselves this: does Le-Hev-Hev really care what the young man scrawls in the sand? Is the test an artistic one? Is life really a matter of graphic design?

The message of the Melanesian initiation legend is surely not a test of memory or art, but the challenge of facing Le-Hev-Hev – of facing your monsters, your worst fears.

(adapted from Kellehear, 2000: 51–4)

The Rehearsal (a trilogy) – Pigeon Theatre's trilogy of performance works on playing dead – is a theatrical set of stories about coming to grips with the age-old problem of mortality, of our inexorable journey towards death. Because *The Rehearsal* is a collaborative performance – an interaction between actors and audiences in the production of narrative and script – the act of 'imagining my or your death' rather remarkably mirrors the tensions between an historically early way of relating to dying and death and a more recent directed and controlled style of dying and death that we commonly see today. The basic human need, that is the cross-cultural need, to 'face our monsters' is not addressed at a deep psychological level by populating our towns and cities with doctors or stories of miracle cures but rather more prosaically, by the personal act of imagining the worst that can happen to each of us, perhaps repeatedly. This can prepare us and therefore afford us a certain kind of protection that any kind of preparedness gives those who 'brace themselves' for events and experiences they cannot precisely predict but know will happen (e.g. job interviews, relationship breakdowns, illness). Even those who display or express a magical style of thinking – that imagining the worst will stop that thing from happening – are afforded a preparedness that escapes those who choose a more denying emotional style.

Imagining dying and death has ancient roots in all human societies, for at least 2 million years, and much of that imagining has been driven by similar motives that drive individuals to imagine dying today – curiosity, anxiety, desire – and for similar social reasons – to protect, control, ward off, or learn. In these ways, theatre mirrors life and death, and in this case, our experiences of dying. In this chapter, I will provide a critical reflection on the narrative parallels between the theatrical expression of dying and death and the historical and societal record of our actual behaviour during these experiences. I want to emphasize, to underline as it were, the ever-present tensions between personal imagination/experience and the material and ideological intrusions that shape that inner experience, tensions that are often both paradoxical and invisible. These tensions exist in the world of society and its direct reflection – the world of artistry and performance.

A social history of dying

It might seem strange, even counter-intuitive, to think about a 'social history' of 'dying'. Most people will think about dying as a physical/organic process and believe that any 'history' of dying must be as long as the existence of biological organisms themselves. But this is not the way I am employing the term 'dying'. In the social sciences, as opposed to the biological sciences, dying refers to the more recent experience of being *aware that death is immanent*. This conscious dimension of the experience of death and dying – in the context of zoology – is believed to be confined to the 'higher' order of animals. And in that world, we must make a distinction between the awareness of death and the ability to anticipate dying. Awareness of death is common among certain insects and fish. Some fish, for example, are able to mimic death as both a defence against prey but also as their own way of luring potential victims closer so that they may feed off them (Kellehear, 2007: 12–15).

Feigning death is not confined to fish but is also observed in more complex animals such as frogs, opossum and snakes to mention only a few. The quiescence skills of 'feigning death' are regarded as an adaptation by certain animals that recognize, at some deep biological level, that struggle can incite a kill by their predators. Looking dead, pretending to be dead or 'playing' dead is a piece of animal 'theatre', as it were, that both recognises death *and* uses this as a device to avoid it or to prepare for it in others. This is the biological basis of our own basic responses to death. And although the overwhelming majority of animals use their understanding of death to avoid it, there are other uses for this knowledge too. Recognising death also permits complex animals to grieve for their own, helping them to adjust to loss and to recognise when to stay and when to leave. This applies particularly to animals that form emotional attachments to each other – their mates and offspring but also to other herd companions. This grieving conduct has been amply observed in horses, elephants and nearly all primates, again, to name only a few.

I mention this 'biological history' to underline one important point before explaining my 'social history' of dying, and that is, that our fear and preparations for death itself have their roots deep in our ancestral history with all animals. Our relationship, even awareness of death, is not uniquely 'human' but rather takes its origins from our development from within the higher order of animals. The recognition of death, for higher animals anyway, is partly protective, helping humans and animals to avoid the inevitable for as long as possible; but it is also a sophisticated and inevitable outcome of the evolution of attachment in all sentient beings. Building on this awareness of death is the more recent awareness of dying – the recognition that we will die quite soon. That recognition of the prospect of death, that social history of dying (as opposed to death), may only be as old as 2 million years, that is, since the time of the transitional hominids: Australopithicines, Homo erectus, Homo neanderthalensis, and of course eventually, Homo sapiens. For these 2 million years until the last major Ice Age, men and women in these groups were scavengers and hunter-gatherers.

Yet, from their folk observations of how their fellow humans observed their loved ones bleed to death from child birth or predation, or waste away from malnutrition or disease, early humans began to understand – not only death – but the experience of dying. In this early simple but reflective way, human beings could begin to anticipate and later, when dying became drawn out because of the pastoral age epidemics, could prepare for it. Anticipating and preparing for immanent death is evidenced in early cave painting, grave goods and similar conduct observed in contemporary hunter-gatherer communities. Later, the long-standing traditional observances by agrarian-based peasant societies from ancient China to the early Americas well illustrate the obsession with preparation for death.

The early social behaviour towards death and dying can be linked, as we have seen, to the psychology (and biology) of fear in all animals. Fear of death is responsible for a raft of self-protective social conduct by primates towards their traditional predators. It makes good sense to understand death if you want to live longer. In other words, recognition of death has survival value. Recognition of dying, that you will die very soon, may be explained less easily in evolutionary terms. The recognition of dying has more *social value*, helping individuals, families, small groups or communities to avoid being immobilised by ancestral fears and to use this recognition to continue to function constructively – to prepare, learn, share and strengthen one's ability to psychologically face death itself. Because nearly all human societies have a view that consciousness continues after death, usually on some kind of 'otherworld journey', 'strengthening one's ability to face death' actually means ensuring that adequate traditional obligations towards family and community are honoured (Frazer, 1913).

In general then, the social history of dying for most people in hunter-gatherer and peasant societies (99 per cent of all human societies) has been a history of imagining dying and death and preparing for it. Before the rise of state-endorsed priesthood – shamanism, mystical rites of passage (similar to the Melanesian rites that began this chapter), and the religious imagination of small communities characterised and guided the inner life of most people who imagined their own deaths and the deaths of loved ones (Vitebsky, 1995).

The rise of state-endorsed religions and priests, particularly in urban areas around the world, led to the reification of religious ideas into 'dogma' – a rather fixed source of teachings and philosophy. These, in their turn, began to compete with individual and community experiences because these more reified, 'official' ideas about dying and death were commonly delivered to people 'top-down' from clerics everywhere. Their spread was designed to override or remould personal experience, bringing both experience and interpretation into the fold of institutional disciplines/disciplining. It is not the place of this chapter to go into the political and social rise of organised religion (see Kellehear, 2007 for more detail about that topic) but only to make the more basic observation that a political and ideological body of knowledge from institutions frequently served to compete with personal experience everywhere as urban and agrarian cultures began to overtake earlier hunter-gatherer ones. Modernity was created in the image of the city so that institutional views about dying have been the key recent ways of 'knowing' about death and dying. In the twentieth and twenty-first centuries most of that knowledge has been church and temple-based although the biological materialist and humanist assumptions of secular populations shape an increasing number of personal views today. For these populations, biology, psychoanalysis and atheism are the main determinants of opinion.

Spontaneous vs expropriated experience

For early humans, personal experience of death as well as hearing about or observing other people's encounters with death were the main drivers of folklore and community wisdom about mortality. Long-standing community observations about people who fell down, lay still, and never moved again were crucial in understanding death (DeVita, 2001; Knudsen, 2005). Changes in colour, stiffness and putrefaction gave observers knowledge about death and dying as surely as their other related observations about how people behaved while sleeping or being ill, or while enduring violence or great personal loss. Watching other people experience deathbed visions or encountering 'ghosts' and other 'spirits' were also informative of folk knowledge in this area. Even in peasant societies, dying people who claimed to be experiencing visits from deceased relatives, friends or gods on their deathbed (deathbed visions) (Osis and Haraldsson, 1977) were powerful sources of evidence that dying was actually occurring and that death itself would soon take place.

Self-knowledge about the experience (as opposed to the event) of death drew on similar sources but could be supplemented and deepened by one's own direct insights from dreams, out-of-body experiences or near-death experiences (Zaleski, 1987; Couliano, 1991). Dreams were evidence that the dead were still alive but elsewhere; out-of-body experiences questioned that the physical body was the centre of all experience; and near-death experiences suggested to many that the journey of life may only be the beginning and not the end of an autobiography. In near-death experiences – experiences of unconsciousness and revival – some people claim to see their dead loved ones, move about without the material support of physical bodies, and are able to visit places and people that populate a world beyond the physical senses. Social insights could also be drawn from experiences of social marginality, eaves-dropping or the experience of spying on others. Being viewed by others as 'marginal' or unimportant has commonly permitted 'unimportant' persons to gain access or opportunities to information or knowledge not normally available to others in the same circle – an experience regularly exploited by servants, cleaners, cooks and maids of the privileged. The experience of being marginal or eaves-dropping can provide personal evidence that, if social invisibility were possible, maybe physical invisibility was too.

From these simple but recurring and cross-cultural observations (Bowker, 1991), many peasant and urban societies began to develop a corpus of mystical and non-material experiences of another world that quickly became the basis of institutional teachings and philosophising. In turn, personal experiences began to be corrected for detail and interpretation with some mystical experiences being 'officially' declared 'good' and other experiences judged 'bad'. The common appearance of so-called heretical views were examples of this worldwide process of institutional evaluation as spontaneous experiences became expropriated by religious elites and then, in their turn, used as criteria to assess new personal experiences for theological and dogmatic 'correctness' or 'purity'. To some extent, we can see a similar process in train in traditional theatre production as producers, scriptwriters, and directors shape and control how 'dying' is to be portrayed in traditional artistic representations and performances. It is not up to the 'actors' to convey 'dying' from the well-spring of their own personal experiences though they may provide idiosyncratic nuance to the physical and social detail of the dying moment/s. However, the broader narrative meaning of death and dying remain firmly in the hands and instructions of the controlling forces of traditional theatre production. In *The Rehearsal (a trilogy)* we find, at least initially, a remarkable departure and break from this tradition as the distinctions between audience and actors blur and as narrative control becomes shared rather than directed by one group over another.

In the above paragraph I observe that we find a departure and break from tradition *at least initially* and I say 'initially' because, on the face of it, the narrative of dying emerges from the initial interviews that inform the broad narrative structure employed later with the audiences. But, as I discuss further below, the themes that seem to emerge from the initial interviews reveal an interesting same-ness that suggests a certain selectivity and bias, possibly in the earlier sampling.

To illustrate what I mean, we see that in Fenemore's previous chapter the outcome of a secular contemporary context and experience is observed plainly. We see, for example, a modern self create a secular narrative away from religious narratives (otherworld journeys) and towards a view of dying that emphasises social marginality (a narrative view of self watching from the margins of the central experience) and materiality (the narrative centres on events in *this* world and continuity of self – no mention of physical or spiritual transformation). I doubt a repeat of this result would occur with an interview sample of devoted Irish Catholics or rural peasants in Ecuador. The 'knowledge' of dying that is used in the construction of 'imagined dying' tends to draw for its internal 'psychological materials' mainly from *this world* observations of watching 'the other' die. In other words, this is a very culture-specific perspective on death and dying.

I imagine my sister and her husband dying in a car crash and I have to look after their children as if they were my own for the rest of their lives.

(Anna in *Clinging On*)

I imagine that you will die in a car crash, in a blue Ford Escort … Or that you are murdered horrifically and run to me dying, or that you are struck by lightning….

(Jonnie in *Clinging On*)

72

I imagine myself dying heroically. I'm going to die anyway, so why not die heroically?

(Peter in *Death Rattle*)

I'm heroically walking to my car, being struck down by lightning….

(Anna in *Clinging On*)

a tree fell on my car.

(Louise in *Happy Hour*)

These are not really experiences of dying but descriptions of events that one inserts oneself into. At best, audiences might speak about being imaginatively 'present' during one's own funeral, hearing the speeches, music or service. Here, as in the other cases, we observe a continuity of self within the trauma and its aftermath. There is no traditional 'otherworld journey' because as Fenemore observes (p. 13) "the otherworld journey is unknown".

In fact, the other world journey is not unknown to most of us, but is – for a minority of the world's secular population – simply denied. Among the educated in affluent societies, there is no 'otherworld' so concepts of dying must be confined to imaginings that are material, traumatic or loss-centred. They are also ego(self)centric (Becker, 1972, 1973). Without a concern for a future they cannot imagine, in a world beyond they cannot imagine, encountering gods they cannot imagine, the material for a story about death and dying of the self must confine itself to … well … the self! As one of Fenemore's respondents put it: "So it's not about visualising how, it's less concerned with how they're dying, more concerned with me!" (Anna in *Clinging On*).

This current sociological context of personal imagination highlights the problem that Fenemore describes when discussing and debating the difference between the 'real' and the 'imagined'. In cultural terms, it is never clear if such a distinction can be made psychologically or philosophically. Personal imagination tends to compulsively attach itself to in-the-world content – available ideas and previous experiences of self and others. In a contemporary bar in England or California, the personal imaginations of the audience will commonly gravitate towards one of the two main social influences: a material, non-religious secularism – often supported by dominant medical ideas; or a frankly religious set of ideas drawn from churches, temples or New Age media.

Traditional ideas about the 'other world journey' (eschatology – ideas about the final resting place of the soul) or the 'non-existence' (materialism) of such a world have been expropriated – co-opted if you will – by the dominant social institutions of the day – usually religion or medicine (Kellehear, 1996). This does not mean that these are the *only* sources for personal imagination. Clearly, individuals do have unique experiences from their own near-death, out-of-body and dream experiences as they have always done. This has not changed as indeed research into these experiences over the last thirty years has demonstrated (Holden, Greyson and James, 2009). We need not dwell on whether these experiences may be explained psychologically or neurologically. For the moment, we will confine ourselves to their experiential reality, not their ultimate causes.

People continue to have unusual mystical or altered states in matters to do with death and dying but such experiences are highly contested by the key institutions of the day. In other words, dominant social institutions still claim to arbitrate over whether these experiences are 'real' or whether such independently derived experiences are heretical, that is 'imagined', 'delusions' or 'altered states'. These kinds of social evaluations apply whether we are speaking about imagined dying in secular terms as trauma and loss ('unresolved grief?', 'subconscious fears?') or in otherworld terms ('New Age ideas?', 'religious delusions?'). The voices found in Fenemore's chapter seem to fall more into the secular order of narratives. If *The Rehearsal (a trilogy)* were to be performed 100 years ago, those voices would tell us more about an otherworld journey than we might learn about today. Either way, in terms of culture and theatre, imagining death and dying – anticipating it and preparing for it – remains imbedded in the dominant narratives we derive from religion or medicine while any unique personal experience and interpretation struggles for voice, especially for individual voice. In this context we must ask: can there really be a 'culture-free' voice?

The invisible *mise-en-scène*

This final question delivers us to the doorstep of others: what is the difference between a personal act of imagining death and the mere unconscious acceptance of a received interpretation of death constructed for us, made on our behalf, one prepared 'earlier', so to speak? In other words, when we say, as Fenemore asserts, there are 'no props', 'no design', 'no beautiful images created', we need to ask – can this really be true? Is this theatre's version of the myth of the 'noble savage' – a mythical figure untouched by civilising/cultural/ideological influences about death and dying? What might be the 'props' or 'design' in a theatrical environment free of paint, cloth and board so integral to our usual encounter with a 'stage'?

Clearly, each audience, like each jury, each mob or each group of spectators brings to events and experiences before them a collection of values, attitudes and emotional predispositions. How these respond in theatre, or court, or streetscape, or sporting event, respectively, will depend on what is put before their attention. In theatre, both physical stage (backdrops, props) and metaphysical stage (music, lighting) help shape, influence and mould audience reaction. These aspects of *mise-en-scène* should support both the central story unfolding as well as the power and influence of the script and acting.

In *The Rehearsal (a trilogy)* the traditional aspects of *mise-en-scène* take a back seat – as indeed does any preconceived driving narrative from the producers – and audience predisposition is encouraged to take an active steering role in the production. (This shift is the basis of Fenemore's earlier assertion about the 'absence' of props or design.) However, the result is – not a triumph of spontaneity over expropriated themes – but rather a less organised and predictable expropriation of ideas as these emerge from the different audiences. In other words, the dominating ideas about death emerge, not from a traditional preconceived script or narrative, but simply from a different source. In this way, the actual source of the expropriated ideas or narratives have merely switched places. In doing so, the themes about rehearsing death and dying certainly come forth from the audience and from the earlier interviews, but no more or less developed as a preconceived narrative, and therefore certainly *no less reflective of the dominant debates and ideologies about death and dying*.

The direction and repetition that subsequently occurs – even with audience permission and participation – helps 'tame' death for sure, in the sense that the earlier ideas about 'rehearsing death' begin their journey of becoming reified – with permission of all participants. Such steps do in fact 'establish' an audience/actor 'truth' about dying and death that fixes and privileges a notion of death and dying above others (others they might make on other occasions). This is – *in situ* – exactly the sociological process that community ideas have historically undergone. But this process does not happen prior to editing, *mise-en-scène* and composition – except in the sense that earlier, hidden processes become overt and apparent some time later. These processes worked through by earlier selections, choices and organised repetition (the earlier psychological constructions of a received *mise-en-scène*, as it were) become, later, obvious and recognisable (i.e. overt, more public in their appearances). This makes the explicit, later editing, timing and placement, if not actually preconceived then at least predetermined, and therefore a logical outcome of earlier less explicit choices and arrangements. We see the same re-figured processes evolve in our current historical context.

In our present historical circumstances the obsession with the 'right time to die' is an outcome of earlier choices about professional control, the privileging of institutional care, and the development of an obsession with medical rescue. Urban societies have privileged professional care in all areas of their social life – education, health care, spirituality, governance and warfare – in contrast to earlier hunter-gatherer societies where nearly all the principal social and cultural functions were shared or share-managed. The success of urban societies has been based on specialisation, and to specialise has meant that one claims expertise and authority in one area but then must surrender experience in most other areas. The rise of the doctor, the cleric, the soldier, the farmer, the teacher and the lawyer has helped modern societies by making them efficient, but it has also led to a professionalisation of everyday life including death. To be dying, one must have cancer, AIDS or a motor neurone disease. Ageing, having a bad heart, or being in a nursing home is not 'dying'.

We can easily see this in our common attitude towards hospices (places where people 'die') versus our attitude towards nursing homes (places where people who are chronically ill get round the clock nursing care). *Both* places are places where 'people die'. One (hospice) is a source of special medical care (palliative medicine) because 'dying' happens there; and the other (nursing home) receives little or no palliative medicine because people are just 'getting old'. Yet the medical needs of nursing home residents may be equal to or greater than those who are resident in hospices.

Such decisions and policies about care *and* the public attitudes about who is and who is not 'a dying person' are outcomes of earlier professional discourses about legitimate versus deviant behaviours/clients, and when and what should be regarded as 'dying'. 'Dying' people have cancer or AIDS and they should be old. But old people without either are not legitimately dying. Children with AIDS or the poor in Africa have 'life-threatening illnesses' or are 'special' or are in need of better HIV care (not palliative care) for example. These previous examples are of people who are not routinely considered to be 'dying' – yet clinically or in epidemiological terms, they really are. The obsession with 'timing' death then is an outcome of 'taming' death – of subjecting death to medical and other professional controls, authority or criteria. The people who fall outside these parameters represent failure, deviance, lack of control, even shame.

When interviewees/audiences/actors create a rehearsal of death that places them at the centre of their story rather than as a lone pilot, pilgrim or traveller inside a construction of an 'otherworld journey'; when the portrayal of death is accidental, homicidal or one that focuses on personal grief and loss, we are seeing an imagined death whose internal psychological props have been drawn directly from the ideological 'workshops' of the present day that deny religious ideas about dying and instead privilege body and emotion. The invisible *mise-en-scène* is a stage, or perhaps an earlier step of an already placed and reified intra-psychic and cultural set of objects drawn from a raft of materialist assumptions and acted out in a local pub in collaboration with professional actors.

Against reductionism: Interrogation, negotiation, freedom

Does this mean that there is no difference between a top-down, professionally delivered narrative about death and dying and one that is constructed in collaboration with audiences – either on the night of the performance or earlier through interviews to develop an initial 'script' or story about 'rehearsing death'? Is collaborative performance making unable to transcend the ideological devices and packaged themes about death and dying that spew ceaselessly from other, more mainstream, forms of modern cinema and theatre production?

In a metaphorical sense, these questions are similar to the academic debates about nature versus nurture. How is freedom and free choice determined when, on the one hand, much of our behaviour is derived from an inherited biology/genetics, and on the other hand, much of the rest of our behaviour is determined by environment? In other words, between biology and environment, to where or what resource do humans turn to find the power to choose? The answer, of course, is to be found in personal choice and experience. Yes, it is certainly true that much of our individual behaviour is determined by biology and environments, and in that context, the choices can seem quite limited. The chances of you choosing to wear a bikini or a simple T-shirt as daily wear in an Alaskan winter are seriously less than if you lived in equatorial conditions year round. The chances of you choosing to adopt Christian ideas in Hindu areas of India are much less than if you were a resident almost anywhere in the United States. The chances of choosing a university-based career is much less if you live entirely in a working-class village in remote Wales than among the middle classes in the South of England. None of these choices are impossible but such choices and chances are seriously and heavily constrained by environmental influences. Yet it is the micro-social experience of everyday life – the individual person influenced or motivated by one experience, one other person or a single opportunity seen fleetingly – that makes each possibility a reality for a few.

In just this way, the influence of fashionable secular ideas about death, on the one hand, and a certain narrative control in selection and editing by Fenemore, on the other hand, make attempts at narrative 'freedom' highly constrained – but not, however, impossible. Collaborative performance making in this context brings together a set of expropriated ideas existing inside the heads of the participating interviewees and an editorially active producer such as Fenemore, just as these would be delivered to audiences in traditional theatre by set pieces. But then they undergo – *unlike* traditional theatre – a process of interrogation and negotiation *by each successive audience*. Audiences do not actively offer up their preconceived ideas or experiences without reflection, and these are not heard or accepted by others or the self uncritically. A certain resonance, empathy and critical reflection is established through participation *on each occasion in each show*. Complete cultural reproduction of ideas is not possible or likely because the narrative control is uncertain in each occasion, contingent as it is on audience diversity, rather than experienced as 'received' as it is in a traditional delivery of the narrative. Consensus is not an important goal or outcome of audience participation.

Discussion, argument and rehearsal bring subtle modification to the shared narrative, enabling meanings to become more personal, to achieve greater individuality, and to attract towards itself greater reflection about inherited meanings most of us have gathered together in our subconscious. And after all is said and done, *The Rehearsal (a trilogy)* then finally reflects back to the audience their own product – making their original ideas appear reified, almost 'foreign', and thereby affording those same audiences another, greater opportunity to critically reflect on their own personal 'rehearsals' for death once again. *The Rehearsal (a trilogy)* as a collaborative performance-making event centred on imagining dying and death becomes a recursive psychological event for audiences that facilitates interrogation and negotiation of received ideas – including those found inside themselves – and in a series of these critical moments provides the possibilities of freedom and of choice. The rehearsing acts within collaborative performance act as a moral mirror to the audience's efforts and ideas, confronting their 'producers' with their progeny. In that context, the ideological 'ancestry' of their offspring becomes vulnerable, if only for a few moments, to critical reflection and scrutiny.

Our conclusions and the future of fear

Psychoanalysts have long argued that we cannot imagine ourselves being dead, we cannot imagine 'not being' (Liechty, 2002). Fear characterises our experience with death, according to these theorists, so that denial, therefore, has been our key method in addressing that fear. The historical and anthropological evidence has not supported this professional opinion and judgement (Kellehear, 2007: 54–65). The facts are that most human cultures during our long 2 million-year existence have never believed that death signalled the end of our personal experiences. 'Not being' has not been a popular or prevalent idea, then or now. The idea of the 'otherworld journey', of an afterlife after death, cannot be said to be some fantasy born from fear anymore than a view of death as annihilation can be viewed as a fantasy born from a fear of religious dominance. The debate about the mystery of death is not settled in academic, scientific or popular cultures, often to the chagrin of some humanists.

The fact is that a broad fear of death, in the abstract, does *not* predict all sorts of fantasies about survival but rather – the reverse – all sorts of fantasies of death produce their own particular, corresponding fears – personal or cultural. For example, for many people throughout human history, the idea of being judged by the gods has produced as much fear about death as the prospect of 'not being', that is of never seeing a sunset again, of never caressing loved ones again or never hearing Mozart again. The principle we are discussing here is this: *Fear about death is focussed on whatever we imagine to be inside that box we call death.* Throughout human history – from churches and temples to Humanist societies and medical schools – there has been no shortage of suggestions for what others believe should go into that box called 'death'. And whatever has actually gone into that box for me or you – that inner psychological space where a personal image of death will take root – these often very different images are the inevitable source of our fears and worries. It is these ideas, whatever they are – 'not being', divine judgement, portraits of Hell, or rebirth into the body of a mud turtle – that have been the very stuff of our personal 'monsters'. Le-Hev-Hev looks like these, is constricted and composed from these very images.

In many societies, the strong and confident presence of seemingly powerful healers has offered comfort to some. Using fantasies of medical rescue have encouraged some people to seek delay and denial of death as positive although short-term benefits in this regard. In other societies, and for other people, religious ideas have provided comfort, convincing many that although the afterlife journeys may seem perilous (as perilous to some as their own life journeys), there may still be hope, if not through redemption and grace, then from rebirth and regrouping for another chance to live and love again. These options have appeared to address broad social and cultural concerns about death but each of these cultural constructions have not always provided individual comfort, or in any case, not all the time. For many individuals, facing one's 'monsters' means, metaphorically speaking, rehearsing one's approach to Le-Hev-Hev.

By imagining one's own death, or the death of others, some people are already 'rehearsing', finding both personal meaning and possibility in their individual explorations. What are the possibilities to be found in such rehearsals? Each cycle of rehearsal – psychologically as well as in performance – provides a certain confidence to the actors and therefore assists with the creation of personal courage before an eventual, actual audience. And when, in the actual event, the rehearsal does not reflect the final performance, a deeper resilience is to be had in understanding that each performance is always unique anyway to both the actors and the audience – a small redemption in the face of loss. The ultimate goals for rehearsals in theatre, as for death itself, are therefore not merely repetition and mastery but also preparation and courage. We prepare and muster our courage to face that 'divine' gaze – a gaze we mysteriously both fear and desire – that in theatre and in death lies just behind that thin blanket of darkness beyond the stage.

Playtext 2

The Rehearsal (a trilogy), Part 2: Clinging On

CHARACTERS:

Anna, the director (mid-thirties) and Jonnie, the actor (early fifties).

Quiz-Master (played by Peter from *Part 1: Death Rattle*) – on microphone throughout.

SETTING:

Anna and Jonnie are sitting at different tables in a working pub *with* the audience. Audience and performers are drinking beer. A real pub quiz (written by the company about the place that the show is being performed in) with a picture round and prize is hosted throughout the show. Quiz-Master asks audience to get themselves into teams and name themselves, and time is given for audience to answer questions. Sandwiches are served at one point.

STRUCTURE:

The show is developed around a series of scenes in which Anna and Jonnie are play-acting, these are marked as 'Scenarios'. At other times they are 'playing themselves'.

SYNOPSIS:

A couple (she in her mid-thirties, he in his early fifties) create multiple imagined scenarios for the death of the other and the end of their relationship, as a way of

Figure 3: Anna Fenemore and Josh Moran in *Clinging On*
(photo: Brian Slater).

both coming to terms with the potential loss of, or separation from, their partner, and as a way of somehow preventing that loss/separation. Because of the multitude of imagined goodbye scenarios and death scenes, it is unclear whether the process is destructive or affirming.

CHOREOGRAPHY:

Throughout, Anna and Jonnie rehearse some simple physical action or 'blocking' sequences. These physical sequences are marked as 'Interludes'.

MUSIC:

Pub music plays throughout interludes, pub quiz question sections and sandwich break.

AUDIENCE ROLE:

This is an interactive performance text where audience are invited to get into teams and participate in a pub quiz throughout the show. One audience member is invited to act as 'Prompt' throughout the show and is on-script throughout (one section of this prompt script is inaccurate and is marked in this script). This audience member is 'rewarded' with extra beer. Other members of audience are invited to look at and follow seven handed-out scripts (these scripts are also largely inaccurate and include sections of the other parts of the trilogy, with names changed to Anna and Jonnie. The aim is to confuse the audience).

Act 1: The Imagined

ANNA: It's something that I talk about a lot actually and I know why I do it. It's because my father died when I was four and I've worked out why I do it. And I also do it coz I'm quite good at visualisation so um how do I do it? So I find a partner that I want to spend the rest of my life with, I go out with that partner, I marry them and I imagine that they will die when my youngest child is four years old and the reason I do that is that I'm the youngest child in my family and my father died when I was four. And my mother was the youngest child in her family and her father died when she was four years old. So at some level I think I'm cursed. And at another level I absolutely know that that isn't going to happen, but there's something about imagining it that makes the reality of it somehow not so bad. So, for instance, my mother died three years ago and years before that I was imagining what that would feel like when I was given the news. Would I be a student? Would a teacher come in and say there's a telephone call for you? So in kind of preparing for it I also tell the people who I'm going to imagine have died so that at some level they can affect my visualisation, so there might be different versions of it. So it's not just about visualising how, it's less concerned with how they're dying, more concerned with me! So I kind of imagine I suppose what would be a worst case scenario. So my son who's three, I imagine what would happen if nursery phoned me up or my husband phoned me up or I went upstairs and found him dead in bed. And part of me knows that that is a possibility so … um … so I try to … I try to … just imagine what I would feel … and … when I imagine it I don't feel any terror or horror, I'm quite calm in the situation and I'm dealing with it. So I guess at some level I'm kind of planning the best case response I might have in that situation … um …

JONNIE: I think about my own death a lot. An image that I have, have had for years, is a sniper getting me. The sniper is what I'm dodging, the sniper is like me presenting my annual accounts, I dodged another year, nobody's caught me out, Newton is my middle name, I haven't succumbed to gravity, I'm still flying. There's no reason I should do. Like the bumblebee, my continuing existence cannot be accounted for by science, I should have fallen to the ground. But the sniper hasn't got me even though I am in his sights. I actually see me in his sights, I feel the sights strangle me, I feel the gun barrel moving somewhere in the distance as I'm walking in the street and it still doesn't get me.

ANNA: Like being in the movies. Or an actor asking questions about what his motivations might be. Imagining things, endless variations and endless versions and there's a certain pleasure in that.

JONNIE: My rehearsal technique is to paint everything yellow and red, everything, everything. And then start taking things out, you don't need that, you don't need that, so I can see how far it can go, but to make it interesting you have to pare it all down.

ANNA: Tell me your favourite death fantasy.

JONNIE: This is a bit personal.

ANNA: Yes it is. You don't have to tell me.

JONNIE: I don't know what to say.

ANNA: OK, well, my favourite death fantasy today: I'm heroically walking to my car, being struck down by lightning, and being taken away in an ambulance. After imagining my death, my mind flashes to the funeral. I see my friends gathered round, and you, mourning my modest (but heroic) life. I have at least one death fantasy a day. And while they all share an identical ending, it's profoundly satisfying to vary the mode of death. I can't recall whether I've ever been struck by lightning before. This might be a first. We were on a flight and the speaker on the aeroplane said there was a fire in the toilet. We did an emergency landing and you said:

JONNIE: "How did you stay so calm?"

ANNA: And I said I was prepared, if this is the end, so be it. And I certainly rehearse those things over and over as a way of preparing myself, but also sometimes as a way of stopping it from happening. I tend to do it when I'm on my own and when I should be doing very ordinary things like washing up or feeding the cat. But I'm not. I'm filling time with fantasies of me dying, of you dying.

JONNIE: I imagine my own funeral. Those great speeches? The thing is, the catch is, you can't sort of take a bow. And I just kind of wouldn't mind coming back for the bow saying "you bastards why couldn't you say that when I was alive when I could have appreciated it?" There's something that some people say, well actually your mind doesn't disappear for three or four days so imagine actually if you could actually hear all this stuff, "well you've got that wrong, you've got that wrong". I just think it's a hoot: the biggest day of your life you're not there for (well you are there!) [*Laughs a lot*] It's been fun thinking about these things, it's like an experiment ….

ANNA: I used to imagine winning Wimbledon or being a really talented musician or a singer in a band. I imagined being a singer and being an actress. I used to imagine my house catching on fire. I imagined

85

road accidents before I went anywhere. I imagined meeting this wonderful man. I imagined my parents dying over and over again and I still do, and I imagine my sister and her husband dying in a car crash and I have to look after their children as if they were my own for the rest of their lives. And I imagine what my future family will be, my children. And I still imagine my house burning down. I imagine someone I love dying and I think it's like a charm, if I imagine it enough then it won't happen, because things very rarely end up how you imagine them.

JONNIE: I asked my mother to perform in this show and she said to me "I'd like to see you perform close-up when you're seventy-six" suggesting that there's a shame in being seen in a certain way. Of course, most of this trilogy is not, including this point, close-ups. They are depictions, presentations and the use of language is beautiful there.

ANNA: When I think of you dying I think of a body I had loved turned into a dead thing.

JONNIE: My mum said "I still have my dreams. I still have my dreams". She wanted me to know "I still have my dreams".

ANNA: I want to rehearse it. To get it right. So I imagine it over and over again, you dying, so that I can hold onto the meaning of you, which is very different to having an ongoing conversation with you.

JONNIE: I run through scenarios in my head. I hope such and such is OK today when I meet him. I hope, if they're junkies, they're not too stoned, or if they're alcoholics, I hope they're not drunk, or if they're grumpy, I hope they're not too fucking grumpy. Life is always about rehearsal. It's supposed to be spontaneous, that's bollocks, it's all rehearsed. Everything is always planned. Do you know what I mean?

ANNA: Yes. Imagine your own death.

JONNIE: I did nearly die once and it was so simple, like um … I don't know if you know *The Birdman of Alcatraz*, I don't know if you know the film, but Burt Lancaster is in this really violent riot and there's this man whose injuries weren't life-threatening and Burt Lancaster is cradling him in his arms and Lancaster's character, the bird man, says "come on you don't have to die" and this guy has given up. And there have been times in my life when I have been so unhappy and I said if the celestial bus hits me, (I don't actually mean a celestial bus, I just mean a bus) I would have so easily just let go. The sniper is what I'm dodging; the sniper is a very different story. But you should always be careful what you wish for right?

ANNA: I imagine you leaving me and laughing. I imagine you telling me that you never loved me, that you wish you'd never met me.

JONNIE: I imagine you leaving me and crying. I imagine you telling me that you love me, that you wish you'd never met me.

Figure 4: Josh Moran in *Clinging On*
(photo: Brian Slater).

ANNA: I imagine you dying in a place much like this one.

JONNIE: I imagine you shooting me with a gun right through the chest. You're a little shaky but you shoot me right through the chest.

BOTH: [*Improvised: Tell us about your stories – Have you ever imagined your partner leaving you? – Have you imagined leaving your partner? – The actors should revisit, or refer to, the stories told here whenever they can throughout the rest of the show.*]

Figure 5: Audience playing pub quiz in *Clinging On*
(photo: Brian Slater).

Act 2: Setting the Scene

QUIZ-MASTER: [*Improvised: Good evening – Welcome – Choose your team names and make a start on the picture round, which is being handed round.*]

ANNA: Excuse me. Sorry to interrupt, Pete has said I can just say a couple of things. I wanted to introduce myself, I'm Anna, and this is Jonnie, and we're in rehearsal at the moment for a new show, called *Clinging On* – a show kind of about us, I suppose it's autobiographical. I'm directing it and we're both performing in it. But we just thought that we could show you a few things from it, that we could share some of our ideas about it, that you could give us feedback, tell us what to do better, what to cut – you know. Um, we've got a few scripts here that Jonnie is going to hand out so you can have a look at them – write any comments down on them if you like, or follow them. Also, we're not really up to performance standard yet and have only just come off-script so wondering if anyone fancied acting as 'Prompt' for us? [*Jonnie finds volunteer prompt*] Great, thanks. OK, thanks Pete …

QUIZ-MASTER: QUESTION 1

INTERLUDE 1: *Jonnie walks to the bar and drops a twenty pound note on the floor, bends to pick it up, then indicates to three audience members whether they would like another beer, indicates four beers to bartender, pays and gives the beers to the audience members. During all this Anna directs Jonnie very precisely with the following words (we realise that Jonnie's action is very specific, detailed and exactly repeatable):*

ANNA: That's lovely, but can you turn that the other way, do the right move. Make that a virtue. Bend down, and bring it up with the left hand on the knee. Turn the other way, down on the bend, with the elbow. I think it would look better without, so it's just left arm over the right arm and bring it the wrong way. Down again, immediately wriggle and come up [*laughs*]. And after that it's point, point turn, and you turn the wrong way. Lovely, but can you make it even more specific [*clap, clap*]. So it's the left hand and bring it round. And with the right extend, and again with the right extend, and again with the right extend. But don't go off balance. Everything you do must come back to the balance position so don't go off balance. [*She has come quite close to Jonnie.*]

Figure 6: Anna Fenemore in *Clinging On*
(photo: Brian Slater).

JONNIE:	Not too close.
ANNA:	Sorry!
JONNIE:	I hate that bit. I hate doing all that physical stuff. It just feels really ridiculous.
ANNA:	It's great, it's really funny. You look really good in it. Very funny.
JONNIE:	Funny would be a comedy trip [*he does a Jacques Tati style comedy trip*] or one of these … [*he steps over a pretend obstacle on floor*].
ANNA:	No, that's all a bit too theatrical for me.

JONNIE: What's wrong with theatrical? That's why we're all here. A love of the theatre … That's why I'm here. That's why I'm an actor. I remember taking my mum to a show in Manchester. A lovely theatre, red plush curtains, a show about a couple, a man and a woman falling in love. In the interval I took my mum into the bar for a tab (it was when you could smoke inside then) and she was having a great time. A great time. But when we went back to our seats, I saw that there was somebody sitting in my seat. When I got closer I realised it was the woman from the show – the actress from the show – she was sitting in my seat. Actually she looked a lot like you. I said to her "What are you doing in my seat?" She said:

ANNA: [*she is sitting in his seat*] "I saw you from on stage and I thought I'd just come down and say hello".

JONNIE: And with that she stood up and as she walked away she gave me a piece of paper with the number …

ANNA: [*Anna gives her phone number as she stands up and goes to order two drinks from the bar.*]

ANNA: And that's really true Jonnie? That really happened?

JONNIE: Yes.

[*Music, Anna and Jonnie dance – He begins to move in close and gets a bit too intimate – She pulls away.*]

ANNA: You know the bit in the show where we talk about how your contract doesn't say that we'll end up in bed together? For the sake of the show I understand why we're doing it but at the same time I'm feeling a little uncomfortable, a little emotionally bereft. Dangerously so. You're doing too good a job of making me *think* we're having an affair so cut it out Jonnie.

Goodbye Scenario 1:

ANNA: Hello, Jonnie.

JONNIE: [*in a bad Russian accent*] Hello, Anna.

ANNA: I came back. I know you didn't want me to.

JONNIE: I never wanted to see you again.

ANNA: What did you expect me to do? Run away without any fuss. Run away from you for always? Run away? Leave you here alone?

JONNIE: It's no use, Anna.

ANNA: Please, Jonnie. It needn't be this difficult.

JONNIE: Why did you come all this way for nothing?

ANNA: I came because I'm your wife.

JONNIE: I'm not the husband you deserve. With me you have nothing ahead of you.

ANNA: I could be here with you.

JONNIE: Never.

ANNA: Please, Jonnie.

JONNIE: Now listen to me. Listen carefully. You don't know me. You don't know who I am or what I'm capable of. You don't know my family. You don't know my life, my history, my childhood, my favourite things, the age I was when I first hit a man, when I first spoke your name, when I first drank beer, or vodka, when I first wished that you were no longer in my life, when I first pretended that you were dead. I want you to pretend that I'm a dead man. I want you to pretend that you're standing on my grave. I want you to pretend that you don't love me any more. Anna you're still a young woman. Don't waste your life waiting for me.

ANNA: [*nods*] Alright, Jonnie.

JONNIE: Go on back home, and start a new life, without me.

ANNA: Alright, Jonnie.

JONNIE: You're still a young woman. Don't waste your life waiting for a man that doesn't love you.

ANNA: Goodbye, Jonnie.

JONNIE: Goodbye, Wife.

QUIZ-MASTER: QUESTION 2

ANNA: Why did we come here tonight, Jonnie?

JONNIE: We had a long day rehearsing.

ANNA: Yes, that's because you turned up late.

JONNIE: I already said I was sorry. And I wanted you to meet my friends [*indicates a table of men in the bar*], and to meet Pete. Pete likes you.

ANNA: Does he?

JONNIE: I like you.

ANNA: Are you falling in love with me, Jonnie? [*she is very close to him*]

JONNIE: No, no, no, no … Of course I am, Anna.

ANNA: Stop that, stop playing games with me. I don't know where I stand.

JONNIE: You love playing games, Anna, that's what this is all about, playing some weird game with me.

ANNA: Cut it out, Jonnie, I'm not in the mood.

Goodbye Scenario 2:

JONNIE: [*in a bad American accent sings 'Makin' Whoopee', and hands Anna a bunch of imaginary flowers*]

ANNA: Have you been to the garage? [*throws 'flowers' on the floor*]

JONNIE: [*in a bad American accent*] What a horrible thing to do to those flowers.

ANNA: Is that what they are?

JONNIE: Yes.

ANNA: From the graveyard?

JONNIE: Nope.

ANNA: From the neighbours?

JONNIE: Nope.

ANNA: But you nicked them yes?

JONNIE: Yes, but that's hardly the point …

ANNA: Why?

JONNIE: Well, whether I nicked them or not, the outcome is hardly a point of suspense (they're here now in my hand, or they would have been had you not rudely thrown them on the ground), and it would, of course, be disingenuous of me to present the outcome as such …

ANNA: No, not why is that hardly the point. Why did you nick them?

JONNIE: Well, you look so beautiful tonight, and I wanted to show you how much I adore you – every tiny corpuscle of you. You're a miracle to me. Not miracle like in a religious way, but miracle as in magical, as in demanding, as in asking too many questions, as in always not knowing you are as great as you actually are, as in a man walking on the moon, as in a mirror shattering, as in a child playing dead, as in a lover pretending to be asleep, as in mushrooms, as in daylight, as in walking up a mountain, as in an undulating dream, as in sudden leaps of consciousness, as in small acts of betrayal, and large acts of betrayal.

ANNA: I've never betrayed you.

JONNIE: No. But you probably will. At some point.

ANNA: Maybe.

JONNIE: [*drops the accent*] Good to get that off my chest. I'm usually not that articulate.

ANNA: You're not, are you? Usually you're full of self-doubt, lack of art-ic-ulace? articulace? articulate-ness? articulacy?

JONNIE: Articulation?

ANNA: No but you say articulacy.

JONNIE: Do you? I thought you say 'lack of articulation'.

ANNA: No that's about body movements …

JONNIE: No, as in you can't articulate.

ANNA: Yes, articulate. Articulacy.

JONNIE: But isn't it? Isn't it? I thought it was articulation.

ANNA: No, articulation is like in lorries.

JONNIE: No, it's both things, no no it's both things.

ANNA: It's both things but that's different though, articulation is about separation, that's what the lorry does. It's about separating the front bit from the back bit. So articulation of a limb, the hand from the arm.

JONNIE: Well OK, that's three things. Are you sure?

ANNA: Well you wouldn't say articulation in relation to speech, you'd say 'articulate', 'articulateness', 'articulacy', 'articulate'.

JONNIE: I think its 'articulation' but anyway that's hardly the point.

ANNA: What's hardly the point?

JONNIE: My inarticulateness.

ANNA: OK, your inarticulateness?

JONNIE: Yes?

ANNA: Lack of articulateness? Inarticulate. Lack of articulacy?

JONNIE: My inability to articulate.

ANNA: That's still not right. Anyway … with that in mind, where do you think that comes from?

JONNIE: [*accent slowly comes back*] When I was much younger I stopped speaking. I think I was six and for quite a period of time I didn't speak, I think it was linked to possibly a kind of depression of some description. I'd been thinking about my parents dying, they were away a lot and I'd imagine them never coming home, and I didn't speak for a number of months. I just didn't speak. I just didn't talk. I think the doctors looked at me, I just kind of, I don't think I was carted off to the loony bin, I did see a consultant blah blah blah, but at some point I just came out of that.

ANNA: [*long pause*] That is such a lie!

JONNIE: Come on Anna, I am simply too well-dressed to be a liar.

ANNA: You're a liar – everything you say to me is a lie.

JONNIE: You should not call everything a lie, Anna [*to Prompt*] Should she?

PROMPT: But you are lying, aren't you?

JONNIE: Yes, but that's hardly the point …

PROMPT: Why?

JONNIE: Well, whether I lied or not, the outcome is hardly a point of suspense. (She's aggravated by my very presence, and I'm present now. So very present.) And it would, of course, be disingenuous of me to present the outcome as such …

PROMPT: No, not why is that hardly the point. Why did you lie?

JONNIE: Are you siding with her?

PROMPT: Not at all. But I'm not following this at all. Are you *you* now? Or are you somebody else?

JONNIE: No idea. No idea at all.

ANNA: It's just another one of his games.

JONNIE: One more game, Anna.

QUIZ-MASTER: QUESTION 3

JONNIE: One more game, Anna.

ANNA: OK, Jonnie.

Goodbye Scenario 3:

JONNIE: [*in a bad French accent*] Anna, come back. Do not leave me. Why did not you listen?

ANNA: I should never have trusted you.

JONNIE: You were a fool to ever trust me.

ANNA: You are the fool. [*She pulls out a toy gun and shakily points it at him. He advances on her, hits it out of her hand and then begins to strangle her.*]

JONNIE: You're not afraid?

ANNA: Never.

JONNIE: I never wanted to hurt you like this.

ANNA: Jonnie.

JONNIE: [*he throws her away*] I can't live without you.

ANNA: I don't want to live with you. [*She runs from him, he catches her and holds her off the floor in his arms. They struggle.*]

JONNIE: I don't want to hurt you. Don't make it more difficult. I love you.

ANNA: You'll get over it. [*He dips her, it looks as though he might kiss her, but then he drops her to the floor and becomes serious.*]

JONNIE: Would you like to go out to dinner with me? Say ten-ish?

ANNA: OK.

JONNIE: That's where I was this morning.

ANNA: What, when you were late for rehearsal?

JONNIE: Yes, I was booking us a romantic table for two after rehearsals.

QUIZ-MASTER: QUESTION 4

[*Anna is very close to Jonnie – He is clearly getting a little uncomfortable.*]

JONNIE: You know the bit in the show where we talk about how my contract doesn't say that we'll end up in bed together? For the sake of the show I understand why you're doing it but at the same time I'm feeling emotionally bereft. Dangerously so. You're doing too good a job of making me think we're having an affair so cut it out Anna. I just don't think I can cope with this shit any longer.

ANNA: Don't take this so seriously Jonnie.

Goodbye Scenario 4:

JONNIE: [*very quickly Jonnie gets extremely angry, aggressive and potentially violent towards Anna, backing her into a corner*]. What was that about? You're touchy eh? What is it now? It's just another excuse to have an argument a bit of a ruck? You ask to get fucking slapped, you fucking love it, don't you? It's the only reason you wind me up so you can get a fucking gob full of my fucking fist, you twat, you wind me up to fuck, I can feel the blood running to my head, just fuck off out the way before you get into bigger trouble, right. Hurry up, fuck off out of here, go, go, fuck off, calm down, get out, now, that's it fuck off, go, go. You bitch …

Figure 7: The Prompt in *Clinging On*
(photo: Brian Slater).

[*awkward pause*]

ANNA: [*shifting the mood completely*] I really like that we shift the mood completely. So we might give imagined goodbye scenarios that are serious or unpleasant, like that one, and maybe try out with the audience a few options for beginnings, middles and ends.

JONNIE: I don't see how you could do that with beginnings, but you could actually have an option in the middle, *for* the middle.

ANNA: Yes.

JONNIE: And you could still have an option at the end as well, that wouldn't be a problem.

ANNA: Yes. I think it will work best at the end because you'll have to give options, but if you give the options, say you divide the show into five acts, you're going to have your opening and then if you're going to do it with your middle one, you're going to have to do it before you were going to actually do it or else you'd be reproducing the same thing again. Whereas if you bring it in say in Act 2 and then bring it back in Act 5, then people will have forgotten about it at that point rather than doing it actually on top of each other and doing the same thing again. That didn't make sense to me. [*to Prompt*] Do I actually say that?

JONNIE: [*to Prompt*] Is it in the script?

ANNA: Bottom of page 100? What's my line? It starts with "I think it'll work best at the end". Can you give me it all?

PROMPT: I think it will work best at the end because you'll have to give options, but if you give the options, say you divide the show into five acts, you're going to have your opening and then if you're going to do it with your middle one, you're going to have to do it before you were going to actually do it or else you'd be reproducing the same thing again. Whereas if you bring it in say in Act 2 and then bring it back in Act 5, then people will have forgotten about it at that point rather than doing it actually on top of each other and doing the same thing again.

JONNIE: We should have cut it, it's shit that.

ANNA: Yes, but it *will* work, as long as the audience laugh in the *right* place.

JONNIE: And then that would really be the heart of the rehearsal. [*to audience*] You're on now, you've learnt it, so now the pressure's on, you're in, the rehearsal is you … If it works then lets do it. [*to audience*] Have you got that?

QUIZ-MASTER: QUESTION 5

JONNIE: Has anybody ever asked you to marry them?

ANNA: No.

JONNIE: Have you ever been near?

ANNA: [*nods*]

JONNIE: And if somebody asked you to marry them would you be able to tell if they were telling the truth?

ANNA: Yes.

JONNIE: Are you sure?

ANNA: Yes.

JONNIE: Then will you marry me?

ANNA: A big fear for me is to be married and become unmarried, failure in marriage would destroy me. I see younger people gleefully jump into marriage quickly and I'm quite envious of that. I don't think it is too late for me to get married. I heard about a woman the other day who's seventy and she's getting married. I remember my dad used to tell me stories. My dad's stories were born from a grain of truth but to the listener it was like he was flying. But my father always knew where it was going because it always had a basis in truth. My father wasn't a liar, he was a story-teller. I've got better stories that are real than I can possibly make up. But I've got endless versions and variations in my head. You should say that. It's my gift to you.

JONNIE:	My gift to you is my stories, both imagined and real.
ANNA:	OK.
JONNIE:	Would you know if someone really wanted to be with you for the rest of your life? Would you know?
ANNA:	Yes.
JONNIE:	Then we must be married.
QUIZ-MASTER:	QUESTION 6

Goodbye Scenario 5:

ANNA:	I dreamt that you would die in a place much like this.
JONNIE:	[*in a bad Spanish accent*] You and I are alike. We're both obsessed with death.
ANNA:	Isn't everybody?
JONNIE:	Yes, but not the way you are.
ANNA:	I never want to see you again.
JONNIE:	Why? Because you think you've seen how I die?
ANNA:	Because you don't believe me. Because you don't listen and you don't take precautions.
JONNIE:	Because you've had a dream?
ANNA:	I'm very busy Jonnie. What do you want from me?
JONNIE:	Everything. Why are you afraid?
ANNA:	You know why. Please go.

JONNIE: You'll never be free of me. You cannot leave me [*badly misprounounced*]

ANNA: [*coming out of character*] I cannot what?

JONNIE: [*coming out of character*] leave me …

ANNA: [*laughing*] Just go. Go.

JONNIE: My mother was my best friend and I can't wait to see her again. I want to tell her about Eric Cantona and I want to tell her about … Anna.

QUIZ-MASTER: QUESTION 7

ANNA: A pub quiz, or an ongoing quiz, 10 questions as you go through the show.

JONNIE: Songs about death.

ANNA: Longest screen death.

JONNIE: Pete as Quiz-Master.

ANNA: You could recreate screen deaths – John Wayne's.

JONNIE: Crippin, Christie.

ANNA: John Hurt.

JONNIE: My son played him, terrible.

ANNA: 10 Rillington Place.

JONNIE: Did he poison them?

ANNA: No he gassed them.

JONNIE: He gassed them, gassed them and strangled them … I'll bring my son in, he could do it really convincingly.

ANNA:	That guy in London who shoved them down the drains and they found that there was a murderer coz all the drains were blocked.
JONNIE:	Nielson.
ANNA:	And he was picking up blokes in a pub, taking them back, killing them, chopping them up and putting them down the drains.
JONNIE:	"It's about time you went": that's what he'd say to signify he was about to murder them.
ANNA:	In a Scottish accent.
JONNIE:	I can't do a Scottish accent.
ANNA:	Try it.
JONNIE:	[*in a bad Scottish accent*] "It's about time you went".
ANNA:	In a Scottish accent.
JONNIE:	That was a Scottish accent.
ANNA:	Again.
JONNIE:	[*in a bad Scottish accent*] "It's about time you went Jimmy".
ANNA:	Better.
QUIZ-MASTER:	QUESTIONS 8 AND 9

Act 3: Endings

Death Scene 1:

[*Jonnie dies in Anna's arms.*]

ANNA: I love you Jonnie, I don't want you to die.

JONNIE: The whole point is I know I've often seemed somewhat detached but can I make it plain, how deeply and how wonderfully I have been so much in love with you. That my love for you has no bounds. Not very romantic I know. My love for you has no equal. This doesn't sound as good as I wanted it to. [*Jonnie dies.*]

QUIZ-MASTER: QUESTION 10

Figure 8: Audience eating sandwiches in *Clinging On*
(photo: Brian Slater).

Death Scene 2:

INTERLUDE 2: *Jonnie directs Anna in a sequence where she runs in from outside as though shot, and dying runs into Jonnie's arms. He adlibs through the following, and keeps catching and dropping her and throwing her through the door. She is getting annoyed.*

JONNIE: OK so lets do your death scene. I want you to run into my arms dying. You've been shot in the road outside and come running dying into my arms. So, on four: one, two, three, four, then you indicate, and lean, and fall, so let's do that again. One, two, three, four, indicate and lean. Are you alright? Your knee looks a little wobbly? Is your knee OK? I know what it is. I wonder if you could approach me on the edge, virtually coming in on the edge, and let's do it at high speed, and from further away, back, back, from offstage. OK so, one, two, three, four, indicate, lean [*he drops her*]. Good and let's go to the bar, not for a drink, for a little bit of this … not really so take hold of my hands and don't let go [*he tries to dance with her*] all the way round and out and back in tightly and out and then I'll throw you away. But this time I'll catch you. And out and I'll throw you away and catch you. Good. And all the way round and there you go, that's great.

ANNA: What makes it terrifying but also what makes it fun is that you have to step over someone's bag or their leg or their coat. It's quite strange at the end of the show, I've been quite buoyant throughout the show and at the end it takes me a while to go away and then come back into the space, coz everyone thinks they're your best friend and they touch you in the way that you've been touching them throughout the show, but afterwards it's just a little inappropriate. Because it's a bar, people tend to hang around afterwards and have a drink and think that I'm the hostess.

JONNIE: It's your party, isn't it?

ANNA: Yes, but when that stops you have to think, I'm no longer in charge here. And it takes a while to get used to being the same as everyone else, and not being in control any more. I don't like not being in control any more.

QUIZ-MASTER: [*Improvised: My lovely assistant will be bringing sandwiches amongst you – We'll be gathering in your answer-sheets to mark them – We've*

got cheese, cheese and pickle, ham and pickle, cheese, ham and pickle,
ham, ham and cheese, ham cheese and pickle.]

JONNIE: I have a facility where I can see life in slides, people drop in as if they
are on parachutes. I haven't seen them for twenty years, they slide in.
And I expect to see them then that same day, and I do see them. And
I'm very comfortable with that. It used to frighten me to see events
ahead of me, of them coming down the road there. I see so many
things like a corner, a hedge and a gate open and you're standing
there, and I've seen it four or five years ago. And you'll say:

ANNA: "What's wrong?"

JONNIE: "Wait till you see this round the corner".

ANNA: "What?"

JONNIE: "The gate. I've seen this before". And once you were driving me home
and you said:

ANNA: "What kind of car do you drive?"

JONNIE: And I was saying and I held and I said "this one here" and it was a
blue van, Ford, exactly the same model as mine, coming the other
way and I hadn't seen it because I couldn't have seen it, and I said
"wait, wait, wait, there it is" and you said:

ANNA: "What?"

JONNIE: And then it came and you said:

ANNA: "How did you do that?"

JONNIE: And I saw round the next corner the smoking remains of a mangled
blue Ford Escort, my car that you had borrowed, in which you now
sat so peacefully. There are some people can give an answer to that.
I don't know. It used to scare me. Nowadays it's just another part of
life. And death. If we had to make, as we do, this show, now, I want
to know how you would make it, what would you do? Beginning,
middle and end, any ideas, scenarios?

ANNA: I like the idea of the two of us in going-out clothes and us being a couple, we're going out to dinner later, maybe ten-ish, we've just had an argument about our relationship. I quite like the idea of how people working closely together in rehearsal often end up sleeping together and having a relationship. You're going to get really scared now …

JONNIE: My contract doesn't say that.

ANNA: You haven't read the small-print have you?

JONNIE: No I haven't.

ANNA: That kind of added …

JONNIE: Frisson …

ANNA: … layer of something else going on.

JONNIE: I think that's great and it also feeds into an argument nicely, realistic.

ANNA: Yes.

JONNIE: A realistic depth to the argument.

ANNA: And that is what is driving this show.

JONNIE: I can't remember my line …

ANNA: The thing to remember is we will always have a script on stage.

JONNIE: I like that you might get to the script and it's wrong.

[*At this point the Prompt script goes wrong.*]

ANNA: Sabotage. One of the audience is Prompt and they've got the wrong script and they don't know it, they're in a state of acute anxiety, you wouldn't know what to say would you?

JONNIE: That's brilliant.

ANNA: Wonderful.

JONNIE: I don't know if it's big enough to make it entertaining though.

ANNA: There's also something about it being a personal thing – that it just happens to that one person, and they're just having moments where there are bits that suddenly go wrong and they won't know what to do about it [*adlibs this line along the lines of what is written here*].

JONNIE: What might be nice is if you just get the gist of the line.

[*Prompt script becomes right again.*]

ANNA: That lovely thing when a prompt comes in too early and you say "I'm pausing" or "I'm acting".

JONNIE: That's the lovely line, "I'm acting here".

[*pause for 5 seconds*]

PROMPT: "I went for a meal the other night" [*pause for 5 seconds*] "I went for a meal the other night".

JONNIE: I'm acting here … I went for a meal the other night and everybody had a menu, and it was a single piece of paper, and everyone was saying "I want that, I want that, what are you having?" And I thought "this isn't the same menu", what they were saying wasn't on my menu, and it did alienate me, made me feel really uncomfortable. In fact it was the same food but they'd given a different French name for it on different menus so on one menu it was called [*bad French accent*] 'Moulin Rouge' and on the next it was, you know, 'Lecoqoqoq' and yet when you looked at it you could see that it was the same food, you know.

ANNA: So what would be really nice if you say what you just said about this experience with the menus so that they realise that what has happened is they have all been given the wrong script.

JONNIE: So in a way we work backwards so this is the excuse for giving them the wrong script.

ANNA: Yes.

JONNIE: Great, I like that.

QUIZ-MASTER: ANSWERS

[*long and very uncomfortable pause*]

Act 4: The Argument

ANNA: I think it's you. It's your bit.

JONNIE: It's always my bit …

ANNA: Well are you going to do it?

JONNIE: In a bit … [*long pause*] The whole point is I know I've often seemed somewhat detached but can I make it plain, how deeply and how wonderfully I have been so much in love with you. That my love for you has no bounds. Not very romantic I know. My love for you has no equal. This doesn't sound as good as I wanted it to. This is no longer true.

ANNA: What do you mean?

JONNIE: Well they no longer believe me.

ANNA: What do you mean?

JONNIE: I mean they no longer believe me. They don't believe in me. As a character. They don't believe me. Not any more. Not after all that.

ANNA: To be honest Jonnie, I don't care whether they believe you or not. It just doesn't matter. It's theatre. You're not supposed to know what to believe. Alright?

JONNIE: Alright …

ANNA: You see the kettle and you say to yourself, kettle. You see the fridge and you say to yourself, fridge. It simply won't do to call the kettle, fridge, or the fridge, kettle, you say to yourself. That's the difference between us, I couldn't give a fuck what they're called. You've probably got it written down somewhere. Fridge – kettle. Kettle – fridge. Don't confuse the two. Ever. And the funny thing is you're likely to confuse the two, you're likely to call the fridge, kettle. Even though you've got it written down. Fridge – kettle. Kettle – fridge. You're likely to mess it up and then you'll beat yourself up over it for days. I would never mix them up, and even if I did I wouldn't care. Wouldn't give a shit. That's the difference between us Jonnie. You give a shit about 'character', about 'Anna', about 'Jonnie', about 'truth', about what's 'real' and what isn't. And when you do call the kettle, fridge, you feel like the sky is going dark on the inside, like the ground is trembling, like you're at the top of a dizzying skyscraper looking down. Without a safety rail.

JONNIE: After the first word you speak, I lose my way, I lose interest, and have to grope blindly through the rest of whatever it is you are saying, desperately hoping that it will end. Really soon.

ANNA: Am I boring you Jonnie?

JONNIE: Right – let me give you a little more space. You've got a cob on now.

ANNA: Fine, I'm happy for you to give me a little more space, I'm really happy about that actually. Don't worry about that, you can have as much space as you like, fine.

JONNIE: Don't be like that.

ANNA: How do you want me to be?

JONNIE: You are just completely twisting it.

ANNA: I'm not twisting it, you're twisting it.

JONNIE:	You give me a question, any question I answer one yes, I answer two no. Whatever the answer, I am in shit. Tell you what, think up the question again and re-ask me. Without prejudice.
ANNA:	There was no question involved Jonnie, all I was saying was that it was your line. I was left sitting there like an idiot again, waiting for you, and this always happens, you just let me down all the time with that.
JONNIE:	It's not letting you down.
ANNA:	It is.
JONNIE:	It's dramatic.
ANNA:	It's not dramatic when I'm not being given the lines that I need in order to proceed.
JONNIE:	You let me wander half way across the bar before you start clapping, so there.
ANNA:	I do that for effect [*clap, clap*] it's supposed to be like that. Just because you don't know what we are supposed to be doing, because you never turn up to rehearsal on time. You never get here, you never get here on time, and I'm fed up with it.
JONNIE:	I did apologise.
ANNA:	I know you apologised but …
JONNIE:	You obviously weren't listening, I apologised.
ANNA:	Well where were you? What were you doing?
JONNIE:	If I told you, you wouldn't believe me.
ANNA:	Don't patronise me.
JONNIE:	I'll make the time up, I meant no harm. Don't look at me like that, I don't know what the problem is, you know, I was twenty minutes late, it's never bothered you before.

ANNA: Well it's bothering me now.

JONNIE: There is something else behind it that's bothering you, why are you having a pop?

ANNA: OK then you tell me what it is then if there is something else bothering me, you tell me what it is.

JONNIE: Well if I did know what was going on then I would definitely argue with you, if I knew what the problem was.

ANNA: That's another thing that really irritates me, you don't argue, you can never have a proper kind of argument, go on throw something at me … You are incapable of logical thought, you can't have an argument and I can't stand it.

JONNIE: This is good, at last you've noticed that I'm here and that's how I do it, but you can't just try and get an argument out of me. Stop telling me my lines, stop directing me. I've noticed the way you do it.

ANNA: So what you are saying here is basically that I am controlling, is that what you are saying?

JONNIE: That's exactly the sort of question that you ask. If I answer yes, I am in big shit. And if I say no, I am in big shit. So I can't win. So rephrase the question and ask it again.

ANNA: I don't want to talk to you any more. I don't even want to be in the same room.

JONNIE: Today, tomorrow?

ANNA: Right now this instant, I don't want to be anywhere near you. I don't want to see you, I don't want to touch you, I don't want you to touch me. You decide for the future, you make those decisions yourself, at this moment in time I don't care. You can go wherever you went this morning and I'll be perfectly happy. You are the one controlling me, you are the controlling one, always playing these psychological games with me. I'm going to go now. I'm going OK? [*just before she exits*]

JONNIE: There is no hiding place. I cashed in half of my house to get that bastard place. I pay for it, the insurance, the car.

ANNA: Oh yeah you pay for the car, you pay for the fucking dog.

JONNIE: Well I didn't want a bastard fucking twatty mini, did I?

ANNA: And I didn't want a fucking dog.

JONNIE: Imagine getting a fucking mini when you can't even get the bastard dog in it!

ANNA: The fucking dog doesn't matter, does it? It's not about the dog!

JONNIE: Well if we need to sort the fucking dog, we've got a toilet that we can get the little bastard down, flush the cunt down there, oh yes, you come back and there's a fucking dead dog in the bath.

ANNA: The fact is that you didn't want to move in with me in the first place, you wanted to carry on in this nice little space of fucking me and then going on back to your mates.

JONNIE: Well I don't seem to remember you complaining.

ANNA: Fucking bastard. You just want to piss off back to your mates, that's all you ever want to do, that's where you were this morning.

JONNIE: The first couple of times we met you loved my life, you couldn't wait to join me and my crowd of people. How lovely it all seemed. What have I done? What have I done to change? Do I drink a pint or five more than I do normally?

ANNA: You drink too much.

JONNIE: Well I maybe drink too much but I drink the same amount as when you fucking met me.

ANNA: You make me drink too much.

JONNIE: Ahhhhh.

Figure 9: Anna Fenemore and Josh Moran in Clinging On
(photo: Brian Slater).

ANNA: What the fuck does 'Ahhhhh' mean!?

JONNIE: [*laughs*] I wouldn't dare say that you drank too much. How are you
            feeling today my love?

ANNA: I'm fine.

JONNIE: Right, coz it seems a bit early for that time of the month.

ANNA: Unbelievable!

JONNIE: I can tell when you're acting … you'd have thrown something at me.

[*pause*]

ANNA: You wouldn't recognise good acting Jonnie if it hit you in the face.

QUIZ-MASTER: PRIZE-GIVING

Act 5: Playing Dead

ANNA: I imagine you leaving me and laughing. I imagine you telling me that you never loved me, that you wish you'd never met me.

JONNIE: I imagine you leaving me and crying. I imagine you telling me that you love me, that you wish you'd never met me.

ANNA: I imagine you dying in a place much like this one.

JONNIE: I imagine you shooting me with a gun right through the chest. You're a little shaky but you shoot me right through the chest.

ANNA: I imagine you dying in my arms and so I invent multiple ways in which I might hate you so that I will never fall in love with you, so that I will never marry you and so that I will never have to know you dying in my arms.

JONNIE: I imagine that you will die in a car crash, in a blue Ford Escort. Just like my mother. Or that you are murdered horrifically and run to me dying. Or that you are struck by lightning. And I imagine these things so that they will not happen.

THE END

Chapter 3

The Performance of Death: A Sociological Perspective

Carol Komaromy

In this chapter I discuss the way that death and dying can be interpreted through social theory as part of a performance. The accounts of death and dying are based on ethnographic data collected over a period of five years in care homes for older people and present examples of deaths that might be considered to be timely. I draw on two concepts from the sociologist Goffman – 'performance' and 'total institutions' – to make sense of the way that attention is given to the terminal period of dying. I conclude the chapter with personal observations from my father's preparation for death, one which was in many ways untimely, during which he was haunted by the horrors of an experience in the Second World War and which became a prominent aspect of making sense of his own life. Goffman argued that individuals in society are always engaged in some form of social display, part of which is motivated by the need to make the right impression (impression management) according to what the circumstances demand. Here I consider what this means for dying people and their carers for whom being professional about death and dying might be what is demanded of them. This raises questions about the possibility of authentic displays of feelings for those people who participate in dying.

In my thesis from which this data is drawn, I use several theoretical strands to explain what is taking place when people are dying. The sociology of the body is one broad and helpful theme as is Douglas's (1984) notion of boundaries and taboo in her seminal studies of dirt and ritual. However, in order to explain the performance of everyone concerned with death and dying in care homes, it was essential to revisit Goffman and draw upon his discipline of symbolic interactionism. Goffman (1959) used three metaphors of drama, ritual and game to explain how people managed the impression they make. He claimed that people have dualistic identities that consist of many loosely integrated social roles as well as a real self. But more than this, the real 'self' that is driving the actions is produced through performance. In other words, everything is social. He argued that everyone needs to make a convincing impression in their performance, but further, that the notion of performance also extends to the audience. Both audience and performing individuals are concerned to live up to what Goffman called "the moral standards of the social world" (Manning, 1992: x).

The move into institutional care for older people

The implementation of the 1990 NHS (National Health Service) and Community Care Act (Department of Health) had a dramatic impact on the care of dying older people. One of the effects of the Act was the decrease in NHS long-stay care. Statistics show that between 1970 and 1998 the number of long-stay NHS beds fell by 54 per cent (ONS, 2002). With the burden of care previously absorbed by the NHS, now relocated to the community, difficult decisions had to be made in the face of finite resources. One of the consequences of the increase in the need for care of older people in the community was that the available money was targeted at a small group of people considered to be most in need of care. For example, the intensity of home help increased while the numbers of households in receipt of this help decreased (Department of Health, 1999). In other words, local authorities provided more intensive services to fewer service users. Furthermore, as Peace (2003) argues, the post-Thatcher financial changes since 1979 were fundamental to the increase in private-sector provision of care home placements. One of the consequences has been that the profile of older people in care homes has changed to one of greater needs. According to a study by Bajekal (2002) in English care homes, three in four of all residents were severely disabled. While the main contributing factor to this disability was dementia, the physical incapacity of residents contributed significantly to their state of well-being. In sum, there is more likelihood that residents will be suffering from long-term conditions associated with ageing, and it is these who will be further along the illness trajectory to dying and death. Thus, rather than needing rehabilitative care – they are more likely to need end-of-life care.

The medicalisation of death

Meanings associated with, and the way that society manages, death and dying have changed over time. Like birth, death has become medically constructed and the medical interpretation of death and dying is founded on a biological base (Stacey, 1991). However, it is less likely that within finite health resources, priority of medical care will be given to the growing numbers of older people. Therefore, while claims about the professionalisation and medicalisation of death might be supportable in terms of its dominance in western societies, making a universal claim about the way that society views death is contested, not least by the way that death and dying in older people is managed. It follows that while the event of death is one that has to be legally and medically defined, the postponement of death that medical technology offers is usually reserved for younger people. For example, there is evidence to suggest that the amount of heroic intervention that is undertaken to save life is age-specific and focused on younger people.

For example, the classic study by Sudnow (1967) on the strong correlation between the strength of attempts made to resuscitate patients in the emergency department of a US hospital, and their age, background and what he called their 'moral character' supports the argument that deaths in older people are less likely to be postponed than those of younger and morally 'worthier' people. If a death becomes the result of the failure of rescue medicine, then older people are less likely to experience a medicalised death than younger people, since there seems to be a direct correlation between the way that people are valued in society and the extent to which rescue medicine is applied.

Further, Sudnow (1967) used the term *social death* to argue that, in certain circumstances, patients near the end of the dying trajectory are treated as if they are already dead. The notion that lives might not be worth living is based on a variety of judgements mostly within medical contexts and usually by those with medical power, and plays a significant role in attitudes to death and dying in western societies and also the way that people are treated when they are dying. Given that medical technology is an increasingly dominant force in postponing death, forty years later Timmermans (1991) revisited the work of Sudnow (1967) and from his findings argued that in terms of 'rescue medicine' at least, the younger a person is, the 'worthier' they become of being saved. But more than this, in his study of resuscitation he found that age and social worth were markers that resulted in the tendency by emergency staff to marginalise older people. He noted that while legally compelled to attempt to resuscitate everyone in the emergency department, staff made limited and futile attempts to do so with older people. Like Sudnow, Timmermans (1998) found that social rationing and discrimination according to age continued to take place.

According to Featherstone and Hepworth (1991), the 'youth' culture of the late modern/postmodern era is in the ascendancy. They also claimed that youth is largely positively imaged, while negative stereotypes are more commonly associated with ageing. Bytheway (1995) points out that ageism presents itself as a set of norms and practices that take place around people who are defined as 'old'. This suggests a more direct impact on the experience of care for older people.

Therefore, while death is an event for which there is always a legal requirement for a medical cause to be provided, within the medicalisation of death thesis, there are age-specific divisions. The status and privilege of particular forms of medicine combined with a 'youth culture' suggest that death and dying have been subject to changes over time. These factors also position death as timely or untimely depending on age, and it follows that the older people are, the more acceptable it is for them to die and for their deaths to be constructed as 'natural'. Having set the scene for who is dying in care homes and the comparative low interventionist approaches to end-of-life care, I turn to the period of dying.

The theoretical argument of performances around death

Sociology has drawn on the notion of social actors as participants within social structures and used the relationship between the two to highlight issues of power and agency. Using what is called a symbolic interactionist approach within the broad tradition, Goffman (1961) deployed the metaphor of a theatrical performance and I have drawn on this to offer a sociological explanation of some of the death management practices in institutional settings (Page and Komaromy, 2005). His ideas also provide a framework within which to explore the 'social display' around death and how various 'actors' 'pull off' their social roles. Goffman's (1961) dramaturgical principles of performance include: the means by which social actors convey their performance while keeping a distance from the audience; impression management; and issues of discrepancy in which the credibility of the performance can be affected.

Behaving in a professional manner is much more than an act according to Goffman (1959). For him, people have a dual identity that comprises the self as a social product (consisting of social roles all of which are loosely integrated) and a real self. One of the consequences of this is that the presentation of self is both ritualistic and moral. The outcome of this is that the self is socially determined and dualistic, socialised/unsocialised. The self is the mask that the individual wears and also the human being behind the mask who decides what mask to wear. Furthermore, he argued that the self is the product, not the cause of the 'scenes' that are acted. Making a distinction between the true self and the performing self is also a social act and socially produced. In other words, the distinction between role and person is socially framed.

The nature of relationships in institutions is key to understanding what is taking place. Goffman (1961) argues that the impressions that people make seem to be treated as claims and promises that are made implicitly – as part of what Goffman calls the "creation of the desired impression" (1961: 243). By this he means that individuals manipulate their efforts in order to achieve certain ends. If it is then the case that observers use impressions as substitutes for reality, which means that they fail to detect this manipulation, in terms of the metaphor it follows that those people who are making the impression – the 'observed' – become performers and observers become the audience. All individuals-as-performers are concerned with the impression that they make and need to live up to the standards by which they are judged. This happens in congruence with structures, roles and relationships in accordance with the social order of the context of the situation and no more so than in institutions. Since Goffman would argue that the 'self' is made up of multiple loosely integrated social roles, this self, then, is socially determined. It is crucial to recognise that Goffman was claiming that all activity is social in that social actors do not act in isolation.

Goffman's concept of total institutions is also relevant to the institutional setting of care homes (1961). His work on mental institutions in the 1960s highlighted the extent to which people lose facets of their identity that they held in the 'outside' world. A total institution is one in which the activities of work and play that normally take place in a variety of settings take place in the same setting and are controlled by people administering a rational plan. Goffman referred to 'mortification' and 'non-person' treatment as one of the outcomes of institutional life (1961: 24–33). Further, he proposed that the fracture between the life outside and the life within an institution that results in the loss of a social role positions the inmates as people in exile from real life and as such socially dead. This suggests that the inmates are unable to resist institutional practices, with which I would not agree (Komaromy, 2010) and that the only social role that has currency is that which people held before admission to an institution.

It is certainly the case that Goffman's theories on the effects of institutional life (1961) (see also Townsend, 1962 and Booth, 1985) have impacted on the way that care homes (and other institutions) construct an anti-institutional approach to life in the 'home'. This was more easily countered in the 1960s and 1970s when people entering care homes were less frail and dependent, but as argued earlier, more recently in the new millennium, the profile of residents who enter care has resulted in an older and a more frail population with multiple and complex needs. My observations below reveal that the care staff focused on the absence of bodily function (what residents cannot do), which, combined with a varying degree of loss of social status, suggested that the care of older people might be focused on their physicality rather than any other aspect of their 'selves'. My data shows that this focus of care was certainly prominent and also highlights how the combination of chronic illness and the need to 'keep residents going' in care homes resulted in a blurred boundary between living and dying. Within this, the dying phase was narrowly defined as days or weeks. I argue that a narrow dying trajectory minimises the risk of identifying 'dying' too early and inappropriately. While the transition into the category of 'dying' allowed for material privileges associated with terminal care to be awarded to residents such as being kept in bed and receiving bodily care and pain-relieving drugs, these were often tokenistic, and as I show, as with 'living', the 'dying' period also fulfilled symbolic functions. In the illustrations that follow, I argue that the way in which the category of 'dying' was constructed served to produce a 'good death' as it is interpreted within institutional life. Furthermore, the performance of caring for dying residents was part of the dramaturgical build up to the death-bed scenes.

Elsie's end-of-life care

St Mary's House was a large Roman Catholic residential home in the North West of England, which housed seventy residents. It was both a residential home and a convent, situated in extensive grounds at the bottom of a long drive. The home was once an orphanage and over the years and, as a result of changing demography, it had become a residential home for older people. There were other similar homes worldwide, however, the decline in women taking religious orders in the United Kingdom meant that there were only three remaining nuns working in St Mary's House, although there were retired nuns living in the convent and a nun and a priest in need of more extensive care among the residents.

One day during my fieldwork there, one of the residents, Elsie, was diagnosed as dying. There seemed to be a lot of focus on the difficulty that Elsie's 'dying' placed on the staff. In this home at least, the privileges that the status of 'dying' conferred on Elsie was expressed, in part, as a burden by the home staff.

Fieldnotes: Meeting Elsie

People began to leave the staff room and Carole offered to take me to meet Elsie. She told me how individual care staff members become key workers to certain residents, and, while on each shift they looked after all of the residents on that floor, they got to know 'their own' residents and got to know when they were not well. This meant that the key worker was the person who got to know 'best' if 'their' resident was 'not well'. At this point, we were outside Elsie's bedroom door, which was ajar.

I asked Carole to tell me the sort of thing she meant by that and she explained, "Well with Elsie, for instance, she's gone off her food and she's not drinking much now. When someone is dying, the nose changes shape and then the face sags and becomes indented here". (She pointed to her own cheeks).

In this extract Carole used the loss of interest in food and drink as clear markers of 'dying'. She also added her own signs of facial change to these more traditional markers. For her this was a universal sign of 'dying' but interpreted as part of her own experience, and not necessarily shared with other care staff in St Mary's House.

Fieldnotes: Elsie's care

We then entered Elsie's room. She looked very pale and was sleeping. Carole handed me the chart at the bottom of her bed. She told me that the care for Elsie was more intensive and included two-hourly turns, fluids etc. and sitting with her or visiting on a regular basis. On the chart was written "2 pm: Turned and sips of water taken." I looked at previous entries and they were similar and consisted of a one-line comment that referred to what had been done to Elsie with no comment about her condition.

Later that afternoon I noted that no one was sitting with Elsie. I walked along the corridor to the staff area where two staff members were folding linen. I wondered why the linen should take priority over sitting with Elsie.

For the home staff, the care that was given to Elsie was completely different to the routine care given to 'living' residents. Carole called this type of care 'more intensive'; however, no reference was made to Elsie's condition in the brief written notes that were made by staff in the report. It was as if care was given to Elsie because she had been categorised as 'dying', regardless of what might be happening to her. This was similar to the way that rehabilitation was produced in care homes. The overarching and dominant routine of providing a particular type of care seemed to have been triggered by the change in Elsie's condition and her subsequent transition into 'dying'. I would argue that this status passage (van Gennep, 1960), rather than the specifics of Elsie's individual needs, triggered a different routine of care that had replaced the previous 'living' care.

Predictions of death were based on markers and these did not serve as independent markers, but were individualised in that each resident's production of 'living' provided the base from which an assessment of significant changes were marked. While these diverse signs shared common features in terms of being 'non-living', as signs of 'dying' they were also subject to variations in interpretation.

It was not just care staff who interpreted signs of 'dying', residents and relatives also participated in making predictions of 'death and dying' and interpreted signs. However, once the status of 'dying' had been awarded, it was the role of any surviving relative(s) and friend(s) to change their pattern of visiting and, if possible, to sit at the bedside to perform a death-bed vigil. Therefore, once 'dying' was sanctioned by a change of care routines, including a withdrawal to the private space of the bedroom, relatives performed a different role from that of visiting their 'living' relative or friend. Likewise, other residents, regardless of their relationship with a 'dying' resident, were expected to continue to perform the acts of 'living'. These routines were sometimes performed around the 'dying' space created by the absence of a resident within the 'living' territory of the care home. However, this empty space had to be coped with in ways that did not disrupt 'living' patterns. At one extreme demonstration of 'living', the staff of St Mary's House continued to fold linen, while Elsie was alone in her room. For them, death was the reality of life and not a special case, albeit one that they did not want to confront and by separating out 'living' and 'dying' into different spaces of the home, staff were probably also managing the emotional boundary between the experience of loss and bereavement and being professional – or avoiding emotional pain.

I argue that not just care home staff, but also residents and their visitors made predictions about death for a diverse range of reasons. I have argued also that, for home staff, the premium on being able to recognise 'dying' was partly derived from the need to provide the quality of care that could ensure a 'good death'. The activities that I saw following the diagnosis of 'dying' suggested to me that making a distinction between 'living' and 'dying' served other purposes, among which was the need to keep 'death' at a distance from 'living' residents. Further, the point at which 'living' and 'dying' threatened to meet heralded a dilemma that made greater demands on staff performance around the 'living/dying' older body. However, the reality of old and extreme old age, particularly for those people who lived in care homes, was that death was more likely to be imminent. My observations revealed the extent to which these boundaries (Douglas, 1984) between life and death were maintained and the strategies that staff deployed in order to do so. Together with this, and with the emphasis on 'living', it is not surprising that for older people in homes the dying trajectory was interpreted very narrowly as a few weeks or days before death.

While I have argued that the categories of 'living' and 'dying' served several functions, it was also significant that the strategies that surrounded the categorisation of 'living' and 'dying' needed to be sufficiently flexible to allow for any forms of resistance that 'dying' residents offered up. Further, I argue that in a spiral of gradual but highly uneven decline, which was the case for many older and frail residents, the boundary between 'living' and 'dying' was not easily demarcated and, therefore, predictions were difficult to make. Keeping death concealed as part of the focus on life resulted in seemingly inherent 'contradictory' performances around 'dying' and 'living' residents. Furthermore, I argue that separating 'dying' residents from those who were 'living' was problematic in settings where death was viewed as the 'natural and timely' outcome of a long life. It would appear that one of the strategies to cope with this ambiguity, and the blurred boundary, was to keep 'living' and 'dying' residents physically apart, not into 'dying' spaces, but into the private spaces of the home; usually the resident's bedroom transformed into a sick room. This helped to explain why it was that once a resident had crossed the 'living' and 'dying' boundary, it was difficult for them to return and, instead, he or she was suspended, either in a 'state of dying' over a longer period than anticipated, or else, in a liminal space between 'living' and 'dying'.

When I returned to the home two days later, Elsie had made what Margaret called a 'dramatic' improvement, and was sitting out of bed. Despite the signs that Elsie might recover, some staff members seemed to think that she might still die. For example, Carole and Marion told me that Elsie had seen someone and was talking to someone. Carole then explained to me that Elsie is not sleeping and is afraid to close her eyes. I asked Carole to explain and she replied, "she is afraid to let go, in case … I believe in this, it's a sign". I then asked her what it was a sign of and she replied, "someone has come for her".

Carole told me, "Elsie doesn't have any family to sit with her". Some of the other home residents visited Elsie during the morning. Two of them said the rosary with her. Carole confided in me that she was worried about not being a Catholic, because she did not think she was qualified to cater for Elsie's religious needs, and that there was no Catholic sister on this floor to do so.

During the week in which Elsie was thought to be dying, I talked to all the staff members who were involved in her care; Carole, Marion and Roberta – as well as the head of home Sister Margaret, who set up the care plan and oversaw Elsie's care.

The care assistants all told me that they found caring for her 'stressful'. The staff, who were not directly caring for Elsie, but who were affected by the increased workload, expressed resentment that there were not enough staff to be with someone who was 'dying', especially at night. The night nurse told the day staff in her verbal report five days after Elsie was first diagnosed as 'dying', "Elsie has slept well. She is much better this morning. I think she's out of the woods".

Fieldnotes: St Mary's House

After the report, I talked to Carole and asked her what she thought of Elsie's improvement. She told me, "her nose is still changing and I don't think she will recover from this turn. Don't get me wrong, I want her to get better, but I don't think she will". She asked me to help her to put Elsie back into bed. She had been sitting out for an hour. Carole told Elsie, "we're just going put you into bed, my love".

Elsie's paralysed side was much contracted. I felt concerned that we might hurt her. As we lifted her, Elsie screamed out. I looked at Carole with concern. She responded, "she has been given pain killing tablets, but they don't work when she is moved. The GPs don't care, you know, because the residents are old".

I heard Elsie's chest 'rattling' when we moved her. Carole whispered to me, "it's a death rattle". I asked Carole's permission to look at the report book, in which comments about the residents that were considered to be worthy of noting were recorded. Since the day that Elsie was diagnosed as 'dying', she had been the first name on the list and her condition had been recorded as 'gradually improving'.

Despite the view that Elsie's condition was improving, Carole did not seem to be convinced and noted the change in Elsie's nose, which was more pinched, and the sound of phlegm rattling on her chest, which she interpreted as the death rattle. Later, when I talked to the head of home Sister Theresa, she told me that Elsie was "on the mend. She was a bit dodgy the other night and I thought we might lose her, but she's rallied, hasn't she?" This home was one that prided itself on giving care to the end of life, even though the quality of that care might not be of a high standard. In the next section I consider a home in which the staff did not want to provide terminal care to their residents.

Performing the ambiguity of a 'death out of place'

Autumn Lodge was a large 'residential' home for older people in the West Midlands of England. The home was divided into four units. The head of Autumn Lodge told me that this division provided more opportunities for individual care and continuing relationships and was more 'homely'. The profile of residents had changed over the previous ten years to one of increasing dependence, and a higher level of physical care needs. A resident called James had lived in Autumn Lodge for four years and had developed Alzheimer's disease in the last few months of his life there and had been transferred internally from one of the general units to the EMI (Elderly Mentally Infirm) one, which housed those residents who were confused or, like James, suffering from Alzheimer's Disease. There were eleven other residents on this unit.

The stated policy of the home was that it was a home for life, that is, residents would stay there until they died. However, because the staff did not have any nursing qualifications, they considered themselves to be unqualified to provide terminal care. This resulted in a tension between the institutional aim of 'a home for life' and the staff's perceived ability of themselves to provide this. This paradox between being able to 'perform' the complex demands of caring for the physically and mentally infirm, who are deemed as 'living', but being unable to perform this for the 'dying' is intriguing, as if somehow dying and death were beyond them. This gap between policy and practice was evidenced by the resistance to 'doing' terminal care verbalised by care staff in the EMI unit of Autumn Lodge. It is worth noting that this open resistance to completing the care was untypical of the other homes that I observed. In this situation James's death was constructed as 'out of place' and, as such, fits poorly with the production of a 'good death', which was the stated aim of most of the care homes in the study. The following account highlights the way James's period of dying was managed.

Field notes: The EMI unit

On arrival at the EMI unit the care staff appeared pleased to see me and asked me if I was prepared to sit with James and I agreed to do so. They also told me how they did not feel able to provide the right sort of care for someone dying and, in particular, someone who needed fluids to be delivered via a drip feed. One care assistant told me that the on-call GP who had seen James that afternoon had agreed that he needed to be hydrated and that, because of this, he should be in hospital.

This was a contentious issue within the home. I reflected that sitting with James in this 'state of limbo' seemed to be best handled by me as the stranger and outsider. It was as if James's identity had changed from that of a 'living' resident, who had lived in one of the main units of the home, to that of someone with dementia, who was now 'dying', and as such, he no longer quite 'belonged' to the staff/home. The focus of care for these residents was entirely on their physical care, and, in particular, feeding them and managing any bodily leakage in the form of urine and faeces, that is, very similar to that required by many dying patients. The following field notes reveal some of the tensions around James's place between being a 'living' home resident and potentially being transferred to hospital as a 'dying patient'.

Field notes: Meeting James

I was shown into James's room by one of the care assistants; James was breathing noisily and rapidly and appeared to be unconscious. His bed was pushed against the wall and there was a table beside the bed, probably to prevent him falling (I later confirmed this with the staff).

James was lying on his left-hand side and facing the wall and I was aware of the irony of this, since Philip, the manager, had told me that he thought that James had given up on life. The room was quite large and sparsely furnished. There were no signs of James's personal possessions in the room. I was struck by the absence of connections to the outside world such as photos and personal ornaments and gifts that were a feature of residents' rooms I saw in other homes in the study.

Field notes: Terminal care

After just 20 minutes, two care assistants entered the room and moved the furniture and the bed away from the wall – so that each could stand on either side of the bed in order to turn James onto his right-hand side. He was now facing the open space of the room rather than the wall. The staff talked to James while they re-arranged his position. They also talked to each other about what other tasks they had to do that evening. "We're just going to turn you over now James and make you more comfortable, all right?" (This was shouted into James's ear and I noted that he did not answer). Then to each other: "When we've done this we'll put Nelly to bed, I'll undress her while you take Rosie to the toilet".

When they had turned James and covered him with the bedclothes again, one of them poured some warm tea from a beaker that she had brought with her into James's mouth. The tea trickled out of the other side of his mouth onto the pillow. The younger care assistant lifted the chart from the bedside table and recorded on this fluid balance chart that James had taken 'sips of tea'. She also recorded on the same chart that they had changed James's position, and then replaced the chart at the bottom of the bed. (I read this when they left the room). They then pushed the bed back against the wall and replaced the bedside table beside it as a barrier. The staff asked me to "keep an eye on him in case he rolls out of bed". I agreed to do this.

I reflected on the need shown by the care staff to be seen to be giving fluids, even though James did not swallow any. I would argue that this contradictory performance, in part, reflected a tension in James's ambiguous living/dying status. Furthermore, as long as James performed the activities of 'living', and one such activity was drinking tea, then the reality that he was 'dying' could be denied as could the perceived lack of 'appropriate' care.

Field notes: James's death

Throughout the afternoon shift, the same care staff turned James at half-hourly intervals and at 9 pm I left the room for a break. I joined two care staff, who were sitting in the residents' dining area. Rachel, one of the carers from the downstairs unit where James used to live, visited him at ten past nine. A care assistant told me that Rachel knew James well and was upset about his transfer and current illness. She added that it was part of Rachel's routine to say goodnight to James before she went off duty. Almost immediately, Rachel rushed out of the room in a state of distress, "he's dead, he's dead!" she told us. The other staff members also appeared shocked, and were concerned to calm her and to account for how this had happened in the space of a few minutes between James being turned and Rachel's visit. Phillip was called from his office downstairs and, when he arrived, his first concern was that James's nephew "phoned from his holiday at about 8.30 pm to enquire about his condition and I had told him that his condition was stable".

Phillip had not enquired of the staff on the unit about James's condition before passing on this news, but, in any case, the care staff on the unit expected that James would live for a few more days. The care staff and Phillip expressed a degree of surprise that the period of 'dying' was much shorter than they expected, and also relief that James died quickly. The written notes for that day stated: "James passed away peacefully at 9.20 pm".

I would argue that in Autumn Lodge, the dialectic between caring for the 'living' (when 'living' was like a 'living death') and caring for the 'dying' residents (when dying was seen as 'out of place') produced an ambiguous performance by care staff. The care staff talked to James in raised voices as if he was capable of hearing them, while they talked to each other in normal tones, as if he could not. This represented both a formal 'professional' manner and an 'unprofessional' one during one set of activities around body care. In doing this, the staff were both 'in character' and 'out of character', and this latter could be part of what Goffman (1959) termed "communication out of character" (181). Equally ambiguous was the conceptualisation of James's care. Despite the 'social death' he had endured on the unit for some time, some pretence of living could be maintained. However, when it became obvious this pretence could no longer be upheld, staff were reluctant to engage overtly in end-of-life care for him. Nonetheless, a partial shift to 'dying care' (in terms of routine pressure area care and so forth) was enacted and this change in care marked both a response to 'dying' and a production of 'dying'. However, the backstage discussions, which home staff had with me about their feelings, and with each other while James was 'dying', did not reveal regret about not spending time with James. Indeed the desire to have James transferred to a hospital suggested that death needed a more 'professional' setting in which to occur (i.e. it was not the business of these staff).

Of note is that Rachel, who had cared for James before he became confused and was very fond of him, was the person who found James dead. I would argue that, at that moment, Rachel changed roles and stopped being the 'professional carer' and became instead a 'bereaved person'. It is noteworthy here that Goffman considers performers may be players and audience, interchangeably. In this case, the other care staff provided an account about James being alone at the moment of death as they would to a bereaved relative. Yet they performed the task of justifying the unexpected nature of the moment of his death in professional terms. They did not share their shock with Rachel, even though they were also clearly shocked by the news. In this sense, being professional also involved emotional control in order to perform an appropriate response. This form of emotional labour (Hochschild, 1983) may highlight what Goffman (1961) sees as the unresolved tension between the 'real' and the 'performed' self.

Haunted by death

My father was diagnosed with terminal cancer when he was sixty-nine and over the next fourteen months I witnessed his slow deterioration and death. He was not ready to die and found it difficult to make sense of why it was happening to him – as if there was some form of justice involved. This notion of having a fair period of dying was one that I heard from many residents to whom I talked about the type of death they wanted. Only in his final hours did he say he was ready to go – and only then as a result of extreme physical deterioration and exhaustion.

Several months before he died, I asked him to tell me about his war-time experience of seeing Belsen just after its liberation and before the medical corps arrived. He had told my nephew, his grandson, when interviewed for a history project but he had never told me. A few weeks later during my visit, he produced a handwritten account that he read to me. He was one of the squadron volunteers who agreed to take water and flour into the camp. The sights of that experience, short as it was, were very traumatic to him and he seemed to be haunted by what he saw. He ended his account by telling me how distressed and guilty he and his mate were that they could not take people with them, despite the pleas for them to do so. Then he looked up at me and said, "ever since, every time I close my eyes I see them". He also expressed deep concern about how they made it out of the camp and what had happened to them. With help, I arranged for a survivor to visit him at home so that he could see that it was possible to survive such horrors. This was my attempt to relieve some of his emotional pain. I know from our subsequent conversations that he did not just contemplate the camp when he was dying but it had always been a part of his life but one that he had kept silent about.

On the 11th of November 1993, a few weeks before he died, I sat with dad while he watched the remembrance Sunday parade on the TV. I asked him how he felt and he said, "Conned! We were all conned!" Perhaps as a pacifist I should have been pleased that he seemed to be anti-war, but I felt great sadness that he seemed unable to make sense of his own war effort.

On the day that he died, 1st December, without any communication from my mother, I got dressed at dawn to drive the eighty miles to his house. As I was leaving my mother rang to tell me she thought this was 'it' and I told her I was on my way. I sat with him and, with great difficulty, said the things to him that I needed to say and later that evening he snatched his hand from mine, ground his teeth and died. He was surrounded by people who did not want him to die. However, we performed a very sad, but controlled deathbed scene! We were all compliant in letting go of him as if life could ever be OK without him.

Concluding comments

The accounts from the care home residents provide a stark contrast with my father's death in several ways. First, the setting of my father's death meant that there was the possibility of avoiding the effects of the institutional surveillance and control that seemed to play such a significant role in shaping the experience of death. Second, the two accounts of Elsie and James show how, despite attempts to produce a particular form of death, the residents in their own way offered up resistance – not necessarily consciously, but resistance all the same and this required the staff to produce a different set of performances.

Goffman suggests that there is a need for the performance to be convincing so that the audience can see it as authentic. And yet, the real need for the performance is unclear. The day after James's death in Autumn Lodge, the staff on the unit talked to me openly about their feelings on death and dying. This was in front of residents whom they were feeding with breakfast. Yet they told me that they would only tell the residents whom they thought might be affected by the death of James. Thus, in a context where some residents were treated as if they are not aware of the events that surround a death, who is the audience for the death management performance?

Regardless of my father's attempts to avoid death after sentence had been passed by his consultant, he failed – succeeding only in outliving the predicted time of three months. This was a victory of sorts for him. Watching him try to face the end of his life with dignity and the discovery that during most of his adult life he had concealed a nightmare made me wonder about the extent to which everything is a performance to protect us from a terrible reality.

Playtext 3

The Rehearsal (a trilogy), Part 3: Happy Hour

CHARACTERS:

Gillian and Louise (women in their mid-twenties).

SETTING:

Gillian and Louise are sitting at different tables in a working pub *with* the audience. Audience and performers are drinking bottled beer.

SYNOPSIS:

Two young women (best friends in their mid-twenties) are rehearsing in front of a live audience for a new 'physical theatre' show. The women (in dangerously high heels and getting drunk) imagine the people they love dying dramatically, imagine their own funerals and construct fantasy funeral play-lists and guest-lists, whilst performing risky but impressive and intricate physical choreographies.

CHOREOGRAPHY:

Throughout, Gillian and Louise are rehearsing complex physical choreographies – each one recognised as a variation on the others, and each tightly choreographed *as* rehearsals of choreographies (with inaccuracies, repetitions, whispering to each other, forgetting etc.). These physical choreographies are marked as 'Interludes'.

Figure 10: Gillian Knox and Louise Bennett in *Happy Hour* (photo: Brian Slater).

AUDIENCE ROLE:

This is an interactive performance text where several audience members are invited to stand in as 'characters' in the rehearsal of the 'physical theatre' show and are on-script throughout. These audience members are 'rewarded' with extra beer.

Act 1: The Imagined

GILLIAN: It's something that I talk about a lot actually and I know why I do it. It's because from the age of about four I used to have a recurring nightmare of my father dying. It's Christmas morning. I'm four years old. I come downstairs early. Father Christmas is still in the living room. He turns round and I see he is holding a gun, his finger on the trigger, pointing at my father. Sometimes it's a toy gun, sometimes a real gun. And I've worked out why I do it. And I also do it coz I'm quite good at visualisation so um … how do I do it? I imagine endless variations of my father's death, some gory, some gentle, some dramatic, some mundane. It's a way of preventing it from happening, but also a way of preparing myself for if it does happen. A rehearsal of it I suppose. There's something about imagining it that makes the reality of it not so bad, that means you'll be able to cope with it when it actually happens. For me, rehearsing is about repetition and about forgetting. Forgetting any good idea you had before you got into the space, forgetting any previous performers you had in the show, how they did it, forgetting about the old shows you've made, forgetting about other shows that you've seen, forgetting how you felt when you left the house this morning, forgetting what awaits you when you get home at night, forgetting who you've slept with or not slept with in the company, who you're in love with, who's hurt you or pissed you off or made you unhappy, forgetting any great ideas you had in bed at night, forgetting about the ways in which you thought you wanted to do it, or the ways in which you thought you would do it. It's about forgetting what made you want to make the show in the first place and forgetting about the show you want to make next, your relationship with your fellow performers, your director, the playwright if there is one. But most of all it's about forgetting that you might be intimate with the work that you are creating, and instead

135

treating it as unfamiliar, as untrustworthy and as uncanny. It's about forgetting your lines … [*pause*]

LOUISE: I've known people die that I wasn't very close to and it's not quite jealousy but I'm almost thinking; I'm intrigued as to what that must be like, how that must be. And I suppose jealousy isn't quite the right word. Mmmm. I often think about my own death and the effect that might have on other people. I imagine my funeral, so recently when I was in a um … um … um … I was driving a car and a tree fell on my car. A while, about sort of an hour, after that and I really thought had I died? I imagined who would find me. Would the friend that I was going to make the phone call to my mum? Would he actually say "she's dead", would he say, um … would he pass that information onto the police or something like, do you know what I mean, pass the responsibility of that onto them? What would he feel like? How then would my sister, my next of kin after my mum, be involved? How would she feel? How many people would there be at my funeral? What they would be saying about me? How um … how so many of them (coz I've had that conversation with them) would be saying "oh my god she used to say whenever you're at my funeral I want you to be laughing your heads off or I want you to be singing this song or I want you to …". How I rehearse depends on which scenario I'm rehearsing and generally I find myself in the position of having a script in my hand [*takes out her script, consults it, and reads out next couple of lines*], so there are characters, there's a sense of where it's located, um … what I try to do is to establish a relationship with the space to try to turn it into both a kind of an imaginative other space and quite literally the space where I'm performing. Um … so the proxemic relationship between you and me is the important thing that I try to establish. I try to find that through my own relationship to the text in my hand and to my kind of developing character. How much space my character inhabits, so kind of it's already been rehearsed in a way. So yes I do it all the time and um … somehow it does kind of stop it from … there's something about imagining it, there's a … there's a two aspect thing … there's an imagining it that means you will be able to cope when it happens, but there's also the fear that if you imagine it *too* much you're going to bring it on. So that really weird thing where you're thinking thoughts and you're thinking actually … and also psychologically I'm aware that you *can* bring things on in the sense that I've often envisaged lots of really positive things happening and imagined myself into jobs or into relationships or into … and those things have happened. So because those things have happened, I know they've not just happened because I've imagined them, but I'm also aware that it could work the other way round, that if I think strong and hard enough about it, I could actually bring about the deaths of my loved ones. And I'm not sure what to do with that. It's a really strange one actually.

GILLIAN: I think this isn't a brief statement, I'm aware of that, is that OK? If you ask me what my philosophy is in terms of um … rehearsal I think it's establishing a kind of conversation or relationship between

Figure 11: Louise Bennett in *Happy Hour*
(photo: Brian Slater).

you and me. Trying to establish what that relationship is and I think it's about establishing a kind of performance language to share so you find a kind of a short-hand, you find a different way of speaking, which in a sense only the people present in that room at that time will understand um … does that make sense?

LOUISE: A couple of weeks ago I had a dream where I got to the point that I'd died and I can't remember how it was, and it has happened a couple of times where, you know, you go through a dream and you maybe … (I think I was being chased, I think I was, I think I was being chased a couple of weeks ago) and there was some kind of war but something was going on. I don't know, I'm being chased and at the end I didn't … that was it, I got to the end and I kind of died and I woke up.

GILLIAN: There was somebody that I knew at school that I didn't know that well, he died of leukaemia when I was in my upper sixth form and the day after he died we all had an assembly, no, two assemblies, and "Live Forever" by Oasis was played. And at his funeral they played "Live Forever" again, and it kind of sticks in your head. That song will always be about him. And it's not like I knew him that well at school. And for some reason I always think about him and what that meant and, you know, the *tragedy*, and whenever that song comes on … and sometimes I play it to remind myself of school, you know, in that macabre kind of way but I don't know, that's dark, but …

LOUISE: I tend to describe my preferred style of rehearsal as fast and dirty. And what I generally mean by that is that most of the decisions I make about what ends up in the final product is very much made in the space, in the moment, in terms of bringing all the varying materials that I have been … all the research materials into the space and then animating them in some way and seeing how one image might connect to a piece of text, might connect to a conceptual idea and have some sort of meaning for me that I like in that moment. So, I've thought a lot about my own funeral, about everyone being there and it's probably in those times when I'm feeling that, you know, that I need, what's the word? I need kind of reassurance that, you know, I'm loved and that I will be missed. And you can get quite indulgent can't you about imagining everyone being gathered there and their kind of grief at your death? And I get quite carried away. To the extent that I'm then disappointed that I'm not actually going to die.

138

So I guess I tend to rehearse these things in quite an instinctive way but there is a sense in which I am terrified at the beginning of the process because I don't really have a plan. But experience has taught me that the best work or the best results have come from engaging with that terror and seeing what happens. The more experience I have the more frightened I become ironically. In some senses the more successful a rehearsal process has been, the more pressure it puts onto the next time. And then it passes and you think "oh how ridiculous". I don't actually think about the process of death because I'm not actually at this stage, it might be different when I'm older. But I'm not afraid of dying, what I'm afraid of is getting old or getting very ill or going through a protracted period of pain or whatever, but I'm not afraid of the actual … In some senses the more successful a rehearsal process has been, the more pressure it puts onto the next time. But then of course when I start thinking about it, I think "oh no I haven't really made any preparations" and there are things that I wouldn't really want people to find, private letters and diaries. And just having your stuff in order and I often think, oh gosh should I always have everything in order just in case? Should I get my things in order? Or leave a letter with someone who is very close to me with instructions and a set of keys you know? [*laughs*] So, I suppose, metaphorically, it sometimes feels a bit like swimming in at the deep end, knowing that you can swim, but also knowing that it's very hard to tread water for long periods of time and stay afloat.

GILLIAN: I was already playing in my head the conversation that my sister was phoning me on the phone and saying "you'll never guess what happened". And I was also imagining myself as one of those people, partly because I have claustrophobia and I was just thinking about falling over all these bodies and sort of escaping and I was that man when he was describing that. The only way I understood it really was to imagine I was there and imagine that I was falling over those bodies and getting out and hearing all those people saying their prayers or screaming … and sort of it's not about wanting it, that sounds really morbid but … wanting to understand properly because somehow in immersing yourself in those terrible, horrible situations, knowing the reality of them, sort of rehearsing them in your head kind of means that if it ever happens you've already rehearsed it and you're going to be OK somehow. And I really believe that. So I might run the scene through and it's very stodgy um … and it's very frustrating

139

actually coz I'm constantly trying to find my space in the … my place in the text. So what I do is try to establish the basic narrative of that particular scene, and the basic position of the people whose bodies I am falling over, um … how they might be feeling in that scene, or what their responses to each other are, and then just do my own version of that scene, which is almost entirely improvised. But what you find is that a few of the words that are in the text creep into the improvisation but actually what I'm doing is taking ownership of the scene, so it's very important that I feel that I possess it, that I possess the space, and I have a sense of why … of why I'm doing what I do. So the most frightening things for me are the things I don't have any information about, there's stuff I just don't know, those really unknown places. And I think things like death, if I can experience it and pretend I am that person then I've sort of, at some level, gone through it. Which is of course what you do before you give birth, or it's before … it's what you do … and of course it's never quite the same as … but there's something about when those real experiences happen that you think it's not happening to you, it's happening to someone else, or you're in a film, or you're in a play. So those levels of reality aren't that different to the imagined ones. So there's something there for me about which of those things is real.

INTERLUDE 1: *Gillian and Louise 'rehearse' a very simple physical choreography, where they move around the space avoiding each other.*

Act 2: Setting the Scene

BOTH: [*Improvised: Welcome – "I'm Gillian/Louise" – Tell us about your stories – Have you ever imagined your funeral? – Have you imagined your fantasy funeral play-list? – The actors should revisit, or refer to, the stories told here whenever they can throughout the rest of the show.*]

GILLIAN: [*Improvised: Before we start I'd like to make a toast to …*]

LOUISE: [*Improvised: So, we're in rehearsal at the moment for a new show – A physical theatre show – It's not quite finished yet, so we thought we'd just show you what we have and see what you think.*]

Figure 12: Gillian Knox in *Happy Hour*
(photo: Brian Slater).

GILLIAN: [*Improvised: Some of it's quite good, and other bits aren't so good …*]

LOUISE: [*Improvised: It's going to be a pretty big show – Cast of about twenty – Huge set, huge theatre – But tonight there's only the two of us so we're going to need some help.*]

GILLIAN: [*Improvised: Yes, we need two volunteers to play Old Man in bar 1 and Old Man in bar 2 – Louise finds volunteers and Gillian gives them a nametag and highlighted script and piece of costume (OLD MAN 1: Father Christmas beard, OLD MAN 2: Father Christmas hat).*]

LOUISE: OK what's their motivation Gillian?

GILLIAN: [*Improvised: OK so Old Man 1, you've been gambling online and have lost a considerable amount of money and have to go back to your wife later – And Old Man 2, you've been fishing and have just caught an enormous trout – So make sure we see that.*]

LOUISE: [*to another audience member*] And could you act as Prompt? I'm playing Louise and she's playing Gillian. Can you prompt us?

PROMPT: Yes OK.

LOUISE: So if I forget my lines or look at you and maybe click [*clicks*] can you give me my line?

PROMPT: Yes OK.

LOUISE: OK so this bit is going to go a bit fast so you might want to keep up!

INTERLUDE 2: *Gillian's solo physical choreography with Louise 'directing':*

LOUISE: OK so Gill, can you just do it, do it with one hand or with as little as possible? So it's two hands for there, two hands for there, and one hand for the head. What might be nice is if you do it again. Do that one again. But make sure we get [*clap, clap, clap, clap*]. Try it again, can you actually bring your left leg and move it Gill with that one, with that movement round? Better … But we need to somehow get it so that you don't end up in a crouched position, so somehow we need to get it upright. Yes, yes. Clap. Just try that spin again. That was, whatever you did was really nice, I mean I don't mind either way. That was very impressive, but I don't know whether you know what you did just then? Somehow she did it, she came in front of you. Just try that turn once more. Try to get it the other way, whatever you did to get it the other way. I think that was it. Maybe different. Do it once more, try it once more. Hold on. That one. Let's see if you can get it, yes, a little bit kind of smoother but no point of holding, so in and almost immediately out … And the impulse. And again. Lovely … Don't anticipate, let me tell you when … [*pause*] Just do it … [*awkward pause*] That was lovely, but we need to make sure we don't get that awkward pause. However you did it then was lovely. OK so let's do it again. Spin back, spin back, spin back, spin forward, back, go let's get you gone OK? If at all possible even quicker … Lovely.

OLD MAN 1:   Fred's got this old car he's getting rid of.

[*"Live Forever" by Oasis starts to play. It increases in volume until it almost drowns Louise and Gillian out.*]

LOUISE: [*texting on mobile phone*] What pub are we in now?

GILLIAN: The Temple of Convenience.

LOUISE: Do you know what it comes up on my thingy? Convetosed.

GILLIAN: Convetosed. But is that a word? No. What does that mean?

LOUISE: You know when you do that thing.

GILLIAN: Yeah but is convetosed a word?

LOUISE: [*laughs*]

GILLIAN: I've never heard of it. Are we meeting up together in the morning?

LOUISE: Yeah.

GILLIAN: I suddenly feel a bit vague as to what we …

LOUISE: I can't get it to spell convenience, I just can't, this is why I never learnt to do that, I don't want to go there.

GILLIAN: Why?

LOUISE: What? I don't want to use something that spells out the wrong word.

GILLIAN: I agree.

OLD MAN 2:   Oh yeah. What is it?

OLD MAN 1:   A Hillman.

OLD MAN 2:   Oh yeah?

LOUISE: Actually, I have to say I probably spelt it wrong,

OLD MAN 1:   It's not in very good condition like. The engine might be alright. But the rust …

GILLIAN: [*to Old Men*] We are gonna have to speak quite loudly.

LOUISE: And with good diction.

GILLIAN: Good diction all round. That's why I'm losing my Irish accent.

LOUISE: [*to Gillian*] Let's talk.

GILLIAN: [*long pause as struggles for words*].

LOUISE: About the show? No, rolling a fag?

GILLIAN: No that's later.

LOUISE: Something about going to eat later, ten-ish?

GILLIAN: Erm, yes but is it? Now?

LOUISE: And with good diction.

GILLIAN: Good diction, all round. That's why I'm losing my Irish accent.

LOUISE: Let's talk.

GILLIAN: What kind of show do we want? Show?

LOUISE: Show!

BOTH: Show!

LOUISE: And I don't know why we say that together.

GILLIAN: I think it's brilliant.

LOUISE: [*excited*] Show, show. Wonderment!

OLD MAN 2:   What year?

OLD MAN 1:   Sixty-five.

OLD MAN 2:   Yeah the rust could be a problem, what you going to do?

GILLIAN: Good diction all round, that's why I'm losing my Irish accent.

LOUISE: Let's talk.

GILLIAN: Right. About?

LOUISE: OK, I have some questions, about the show.

GILLIAN: [*to audience member*] Well we were going to eat later, weren't we? We can meet you later on if you wanted … to go and eat.

LOUISE: [*to audience member*] Yeah? I mean ten-ish?

GILLIAN: [*to audience member*] Ten?

LOUISE: [*to audience member*] Is that too late for you?

GILLIAN: Actually, we're going to talk about the show. What kind of show do we want? What kind of show …

BOTH: [*excited*] Show, show, show!

GILLIAN: I'm going to roll a fag now. No! [*soundtrack of "Live Forever" by Oasis very loud by now*] Those other discussions. And um … I think at some point it might be good for us to have those other discussions, you know, the ones we started at the opening of the show, but I think not with [*points to beer*] … or with … [*points to audience*] or with … [*shouts to the technician operating sound to turn it off – soundtrack is turned off*]

LOUISE: Nor with er … [*indicates Old Men*]

OLD MAN 1:   Might turn the engine over. Get Bob to have a look at it.

145

OLD MAN 2:   Yeah you could do.

GILLIAN: I see … [*long pause*] … So, I'm gonna roll a fag?

LOUISE: Sorry. [*to Prompt*] She says sorry, doesn't she?

PROMPT: Yes.

GILLIAN: What?

LOUISE: Sorry.

GILLIAN: Oh, yes, I'm gonna roll a fag, *sorry*.

GILLIAN: It's not very good that bit, is it? Could you test me please? Mine's highlighted. I'm playing Gillian, and you're playing audience member. From "where are we now?"

AUDIENCE MEMBER: Where are we now?

GILLIAN: We're there, from "where are we now?"

AUDIENCE MEMBER: OK. "Where are we now?"

GILLIAN: The Temple of Convenience.

AUDIENCE MEMBER: Do you know what it comes up on my thingy? Convetosed.

GILLIAN: Convetosed. WHAT'S THAT?

AUDIENCE MEMBER: [*corrects her*] WHAT DOES THAT MEAN?

GILLIAN: Sorry. WHAT DOES THAT MEAN?

AUDIENCE MEMBER: You know when you do that thing?

GILLIAN: [*struggles for words*]

AUDIENCE MEMBER: Yeah but is convetosed a word?

GILLIAN: Oh yeah, but is convetosed a word? Then you laugh.

AUDIENCE MEMBER: [*laughs*]

GILLIAN: Are we meeting up together in the morning?

AUDIENCE MEMBER: You've missed out "I've never heard of it."

GILLIAN: Have I? Where?

AUDIENCE MEMBER: "I've never heard of it. Are we meeting up together in the morning?"

GILLIAN: Oh yes. "I've never heard of it. Are we meeting up together in the morning?"

AUDIENCE MEMBER: [*pause*]

OLD MAN 1:   Tom says his outboard motor has gone. She hangs back a bit.

OLD MAN 2:   She shouldn't be doing that. I'll have a look at her. He'll need a new one. A new motor. It'll steer all wrong.

LOUISE: Show! Let's think about the shows that we've seen recently that we really like.

GILLIAN: Yeah.

LOUISE: That might be usable, re-usable. Show-wise.

GILLIAN: I've seen a really good thing that this French company did, and they built this huge big steel um … steel kind of a … um … um … it looked like this mad science lab. Um … this big massive thing that was up in the air, and there was a hamster wheel and one guy would run in the hamster wheel and he would build up enough energy for a see-saw to go, then another guy would get on a see-saw and he was wearing kind of all white bubble wrap and wellingtons, and he was kind of going up and down on his side, wearing a white suit with white Wellington boots and he was going up and down. And the other side there was no one on it but it would have bellows to create fire, so every time he

Figure 13: Old Man 1 in *Happy Hour*
(photo: Brian Slater).

was going up and down, splashing in water and at the other end of the
see-saw the air was flaming the fire that was causing this part of this
contraption to go up and up and up and as this ... it was really, really
slow you know, there was no dialogue, it was just the images of your
man running on the thing, your man on the see-saw and there was
this pole it was like a big telegraph pole and it was like it was being
wound up, up, up, up and up and on top of this pole was another guy
who was just stood up there and he was reading, and the pole would
just go up until it was really high, he was, well first of all he was sat and
he was pretending to read, I don't think he was really reading because
he was moving and he was ripping off the pages that he read and he
would stuff them in his mouth and eat them. Now this contraption

managed to get to its full maximum, maximum height and once it got to that height he jumped, he just jumped. He jumped off the pole and he circled round until he hit the ground ...

LOUISE: Was this real? That really happened?

GILLIAN: Yeah yeah.

LOUISE: Wow.

GILLIAN: We probably couldn't do that though.

LOUISE: No.

GILLIAN: It was a really good show.

LOUISE: It sounds it.

LOUISE: I've seen a few things, a few installations, not necessarily theatre. Interactive pieces.

GILLIAN: [*yawns*]

LOUISE: Are you bored Gillian?

GILLIAN: Sorry. [*laughs*]

LOUISE: An interactive piece but it wasn't necessarily a performance piece um ... more kind of visual arts and it's just ... it really reminded me of something ... European. It's just quite quirky and dark ... where you'd go into this wooded area and there'd just be these little booths.

GILLIAN: [*yawns*]

LOUISE: Are you bored Gill? Fucking hell. Tiny little booths that you'd have er ... a personal one to one moment. One might be this clear bubble, spherical bubble with a bird inside, a cut out bird and lots of feathers everywhere, just aesthetically beautiful, you'd spin the ball coz it was hanging from a tree and it would spin around and all these feathers would float everywhere. And another thing would be lots of times

149

you would have to go up high or crouch below, you know those, what are they called? Kaleidoscopes? Those wheels that you spin, like the horse, the old fashioned, the cinema thing, a horse jumps a fence, a man drops from the sky. And there'd be another booth with ... Like an old fashioned bird cage, you put your hands through where you'd get the bird in and out and there'd be a flip book in there and you'd flip the book and there'd be a pigeon in flight.

GILLIAN: Pigeons in flight. That really happened?

GILLIAN: Yeah yeah.

LOUISE: Wow.

GILLIAN: We probably couldn't do that though.

LOUISE: No.

GILLIAN: It was a really good show.

LOUISE: It sounds it.

[*Improvised: Gillian and Louise ask the audience about good shows they've seen recently.*]

LOUISE: Can you test me?

AUDIENCE MEMBER: Yes OK.

LOUISE: Look I'm highlighted. [*whispers*] Look there you are. Can you test that I get the lines right?

AUDIENCE MEMBER: Yes OK.

LOUISE: Word for word. All the lines right.

AUDIENCE MEMBER: Yes OK.

LOUISE: I can't get it to spell convenience. I just can't. This is why I never learnt to do that. I don't want to use something that spells out the wrong word.

AUDIENCE MEMBER: I just can't and I don't want to go there.

LOUISE: What do you mean?

AUDIENCE MEMBER: You missed [*with quotation mark hand gestures*] "I just can't" and "I don't want to go there".

LOUISE: What should it be?

AUDIENCE MEMBER: I can't get it to spell convenience. [*with quotation mark hand gestures*] "I just can't". This is why I never learnt to do that. [*with quotation mark hand gestures*] "I don't want to go there". I don't want to use something that spells out the wrong word.

LOUISE: [*looks at script over audience member's shoulder*] Oh that! You don't need to worry about details like that. No-one will know.

OLD MAN 2:   I don't think I should buy that car. Too much needs doing on it. And the rust. Not enough space. I'll stick with what I've got.

OLD MAN 1:   Right so. What you've got is OK. You need any more parts?

OLD MAN 2:   She's running smoothly enough. A few hiccoughs. Nothing major.

INTERLUDE 3: *Louise tries to get audience (individuals and collectively) to 'interpret' her commands.*

LOUISE: OK so can you just do it, do it with one hand or with as little as possible. So it's two hands for there, two hands for there, and one hand for the head. What might be nice is if you do it again. Do that one again. But make sure we get [*clap, clap, clap, clap*]. Try it again, can you actually bring your left leg and move it with that one, with that movement round? Better ... But we need to somehow get it so that you don't end up in a crouched position, so somehow we need to get it upright. Yes, yes. Clap. Just try that spin again. That was, whatever you did was really nice, I mean I don't mind either way. That was very impressive, but I don't know whether you know what you did just then? Somehow she did it, she came in front of you. Just try that turn once more. Try to get it the other way, whatever you did to get it the other way. I think that was it. Maybe different. Do it once more, try it once more. Hold on. That one. Let's see if you can get it, yes, a little bit kind of smoother but no point of holding so in and almost immediately out … And the impulse. And again. Lovely … Don't anticipate, let me tell you when … [*pause*] … Just do it. [*awkward pause*] That was lovely, but we need to make sure we don't get that awkward pause. However you did it then was lovely. OK so let's do it again. Spin back, spin back, spin back, spin forward, back, go let's get you gone OK? If at all possible even quicker … Lovely.

[*Gillian and Louise return to their seats and begin writing in their rehearsal books/ scripts.*]

GILLIAN: Why, when you … you write your rehearsal notes they're always diagrammatical, aren't they? Literally more so, I don't know, I think more so than mine.

LOUISE: Yeah.

GILLIAN: Yeah, I used to do it, I think it's more about journeys for you. I used to do it but now I can't understand the diagrams.

LOUISE: If I know the general direction, I can then … Piece together the other bits. If you had written … if you had written some of those … some of those choreographies that we did earlier down in a diagrammatical way then you, then you would have remembered them.

GILLIAN: You think so? I just don't get them. I think I can only really try and commit it to memory because going over the diagrams I found I had to keep going back to the place I'd been to because there was so many times going back to the same point that there was no way to differentiate what was where. And there's no way of diagrammatically recording rhythm.

OLD MAN 1:   Well she needs a new gasket.

OLD MAN 2:   Right so.

OLD MAN 1:   But it might stick.

Act 3: Endings

GILLIAN: Right, we've been having problems deciding on an ending so we could really do with your help.

LOUISE: We've got two options. Option 1 …

GILLIAN: I'll introduce you.

LOUISE: I don't think I need any introduction.

Option 1:

LOUISE: Every night I dream the same dream, but with tiny differences. Two strangers enter the room with guns or they attack me as I leave the theatre or they wait for me in the bar after rehearsals and seem not to recognise me. At the end of the dream, they aim their guns and shoot me in the stomach. As the bullet enters my flesh I wake up. It is only a dream. But the dream will be repeated over and over again, with tiny differences. The strangers will kill me every night. Each night I'll wake as the bullet enters my flesh. Imagining my murder and endlessly awaiting it is not bearable. One evening the presence of strangers scares me, they're all looking at me: silent, still, watching. I know they're here to kill me. With a gesture I ask them to wait and turn to face the wall. I close my eyes and imagine that I am dreaming, that they will shoot me in the stomach, and that as the bullet enters my flesh I will wake up.

INTERLUDE 4: *Louise's solo choreography as Gillian 'directs':*

GILLIAN: [*holding a toy gun to Louise's head*] That was nice. Can you … that's perfect. Do one set of turns then stop. Do the correct one. Make that a virtue. Let's see how big you can go … don't worry go back a set. Do it on that bend. Down on the elbow. Come up again. Use your hand on your belly to come up. [*laughs*] I think it would look better without. Any way of having the other hand … up? So it's just the left arm over the right arm. And immediately wriggle and come out. After that point, stop look to that point

153

over there. Do that again, point, point, move, and then you turn the wrong way. Let's make that very specific so all you have to do is the heel so you end up over there. Same place from the head. Can it be even more that you're having … She's, you're not, she doesn't, you know what it is, she doesn't, she wants to go that way, you want to go that way …

LOUISE: Right so I want to go that way?

GILLIAN: No, you want to go that way, but, I don't know … yes … try it again. Can we just make it even more that you're having so, so you hit, then you pass it out. Again Lou, so left arm brings it down so you bring it round. And then? Left arm brings it down, yes. Try it again. Yes. [*Louise is on the floor lying on her back*] Let's make that nice [*Gillian opens Louise's legs wide and aims toy gun at her*]. Everything you do needs to come back to a balanced position so don't go off balance. So point, point, and get up. Do that as a slap before you do that. Slap and then take it round. Slap and bring it round. Ta ta tchow [*'gun' goes off*].

BOTH: And that's option number 1 …

GILLIAN: It's good that one.

LOUISE: Yes but here is option 2 …

Option 2:

INTERLUDE 5: *Louise and GIllian perform detailed choreography around audience. Towards end Louise goes back to seat, takes out mobile phone and phones Gillian (who continues with choreography until phone rings, when she excuses herself and answers phone).*

LOUISE: Gillian?

GILLIAN: Yes. Where are you?

LOUISE: In a bar. Where are you?

GILLIAN: Which one?

LOUISE:	Temple of Convenience.
LOUISE:	I'm going to have to come and get you. Don't move.
GILLIAN:	Is everything alright?
LOUISE:	I shouldn't tell you over the phone.
GILLIAN:	Tell me what?
LOUISE:	No I can't. Something has happened and I need to tell you face-to-face.
GILLIAN:	Just tell me. Whatever needs to be said needs to be said now. I mean it Louise.
LOUISE:	The police contacted me. I was the first number in his phone book.
GILLIAN:	I've been imagining this. I was already playing in my head this conversation. I knew you would be phoning me on the phone and saying "you'll never guess what has happened". I knew that if I thought hard and strong enough about it, I could bring it on. When I imagine it I don't feel terror or horror, I'm quite calm in the situation and I'm dealing with it.
BOTH:	And that's option number 2 …
GILLIAN:	Pretty good too. Let's take a vote.
LOUISE:	[*Improvised: So option 1, hands up? – And option 2? – [they count] So OPTION ? it is.*]
GILLIAN:	Can you test me? OK so that bit's me. I'm Gillian, or Gill whichever you prefer. But yes I'm the highlighted bit and you are the audience member. OK so "well we're going to eat later, we can meet later on to go and eat".
AUDIENCE MEMBER:	Where are we?
GILLIAN:	Over the page

AUDIENCE MEMBER: Oh sorry.

GILLIAN: OK so "well we're going to eat later we can meet later on to go and eat".

AUDIENCE MEMBER: No it's "well we're going together, well we're going to eat later, weren't we?"

GILLIAN: "Well we're going together, well we're going to eat later, weren't we?"

AUDIENCE MEMBER: I could meet you later on if you wanted … to go and eat.

GILLIAN: [*flirting*] Oh … I'd love to. Thanks for that. [*Gillian continues flirting with this audience member throughout the rest of show.*]

INTERLUDE 6: *Gillian teaches Louise a short physical choreography.*

Act 4: The Argument

LOUISE: I like for the beginning for us to be sitting drinking beer together, then one of us starts speaking and we're talking very ordinarily about rehearsing and it's a very simple conversation that sets the scene but it goes on at length, so that we think that ahh … we're just going to sit and listen to those two talking, nothing happens.

GILLIAN: I like, I like a story, when I'm watching things what I really like is a story, I enjoy a good tale, I like all the ideas, I'd like to tell a story. You know it doesn't have to be a major thing.

LOUISE: No

GILLIAN: A personal story or a short story.

OLD MAN 2:   Jeez it's busy now.

LOUISE: With characters.

GILLIAN: Yeah, but not an A to Z structure.

LOUISE: I don't like work that doesn't address character. Even if there are different levels to it so we don't always know which is the real one and which is the other layer.

GILLIAN: I like a good story.

LOUISE: So Gillian what's the story? Now this instant, you have to have it.

GILLIAN: This instant? Maybe it's a story about friendship.

LOUISE: OK.

GILLIAN: I don't necessarily see us as lovers or anything. I don't really see that.

LOUISE: Maybe friendship borders on these boundaries.

GILLIAN: Yeah

LOUISE: [*clicks*] Prompt. So Gill has just said 'yeah' at the middle of page 157 Act 4. In response to me saying "maybe friendship borders on these boundaries".

PROMPT: "Maybe you expect more from those friendships than friendship is about and it becomes confusing. Or ..."

LOUISE: Yes.

PROMPT: No I say "yes".

LOUISE: Before or after that line?

PROMPT: Which line?

LOUISE: The next line.

PROMPT: Both.

LOUISE: OK so what's the next bit? I say "Or ..." [*clicks*]

PROMPT: Or "over relying perhaps on someone too much in a way that you shouldn't be doing".

LOUISE: Is this you? Or are you still prompting?

PROMPT: No, that's your line.

LOUISE: Oh, I see. So "maybe you expect more from those friendships than friendship is about and it becomes confusing".

PROMPT: Yes.

LOUISE: Or over-relying perhaps on someone too much in a way that you shouldn't be doing.

PROMPT: Yes.

LOUISE: Thank God ...

GILLIAN: So we want to take the audience on a journey but without them over-relying on us in a way that they shouldn't be doing.

LOUISE: On a journey so they feel comfortable with what is going on and they can respond, and they can laugh and they can feel the urgency of where they are taken either physically or mentally. But I really like the idea of after that moment when the lights go down and they come up again that they are taken somewhere immediately, engaging the audience into that old familiar place of the bar and so they are immediately taken on that journey where they don't feel like they're in an alien space but in a space where they can laugh and they can feel comfortable, I don't know the story, I can't think, but I know I want them to feel very comfortable in that moment. But a kind of comfortable that allows them to be taken somewhere else.

GILLIAN: We don't want it to be a trendy bar full of young people though coz that's somewhere to be seen, that's a place to be looked at rather than a place where you are connecting with the people that you've gone to meet up with.

OLD MAN 1:   No, I think I'll stick with the one I have.

OLD MAN 2:   Right so.

LOUISE: We should research this vigorously over the next few days, pubs we like.

OLD MAN 1:   Or …

LOUISE: Like I remember when we went to Anglesey on Sunday we went to that, to that, I went into that pub to get some drinks for us, was it called *The Ship Inn* or something? And it was obviously a popular pub, it had lots of tourists. It was an old fashioned pub by the coast, and there were a couple of old men at the bar and I remember waiting to order my drinks and there were long silences, the conversation was silence, silence and one of them would say something and the other would respond so they would have a bit of a slow conversation. And then they'd stop and observe what was going on around them and it was civilised, sea oriented, boat oriented, car oriented, then one of them would pick up the conversation on a thought going around their head and the other one would join in, so he was going "I don't think I should buy this car I think I'm going to stick with the car I got". And this other man was saying "oh it's very busy at this time of year".

OLD MAN 2:   I suppose it's high season. [**Old men 1 and 2 are finished**]

LOUISE: And this was a slow, slow conversation, so so slow, slow.

GILLIAN: So what if … what if two-thirds of the way through the show you say "I was in Anglesey the other week and I was in a pub and it was totally silent until these two people started to speak" and you kind of start setting it up so, you're … it's almost as though you get them to play these roles, like the two old men at the bar. It's all very weird. You then have me coming in saying what I'm saying now. And I get this big speech to make them feel comfortable.

[*pause*]

LOUISE: Why do you get the big speech?

GILLIAN: You will always have a central protagonist in the story. You will always have someone who the audience will grasp onto and follow through that kind of journey. And I think I should be the one doing it.

LOUISE: It's something about your mannerisms that are just wrong.

GILLIAN: My mannerisms aren't wrong. Your mannerisms are just weird. We definitely need that one person to come through at the beginning otherwise we'll lose the audience. We need warmth. I think we need someone like me to give that. I have that kind of "I'm going to look after you guys, you don't have to worry about anything that's going on, my colleague is going to be a bit grotesque, a bit macabre, but don't worry I'm always here for you". I don't think you can do that. From your point of view you just want to freak the fuck out of them. You're in the wrong place, you should be over there.

INTERLUDE 7: *Louise teaches Gillian a physical choreography throughout the following argument, the choreography getting increasingly violent.*

LOUISE: What do you mean I'm a freaky fucker?

GILLIAN: It's pretty obvious what I mean. You just are a freaky fucker.

LOUISE: Can you elaborate on that?

GILLIAN: Look at you. Really, you'd scare the fuck out of anyone. Don't ask another question.

LOUISE: OK. Then why don't you just fuck off?

GILLIAN: Now you're talking.

LOUISE: So if I'm a freaky fucker what does that make you? You unapproachable bitch.

GILLIAN: Bitch is it? Thought we'd already established I'm the friendly one.

LOUISE: That's quite clear. Why don't we all take notes?

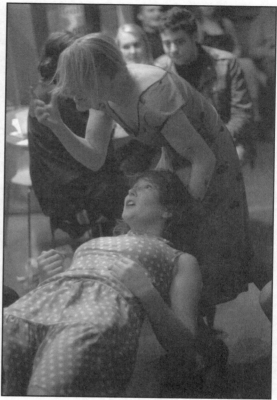

Figure 14: Gillian Knox and Louise Bennett in *Happy Hour*
(photo: Brian Slater).

GILLIAN: What? What are we taking notes on?

LOUISE: The friendly Gill.

GILLIAN: What?

LOUISE: So you're telling me you're the friendly one.

GILLIAN: Yes I've got a bit of a lilt, whereas you're the confrontational one.

LOUISE:	So doing what I do in rehearsal makes me confrontational?
GILLIAN:	Yes.
LOUISE:	Why don't you … look in a mirror, bitch.
GILLIAN:	Good one. Witty. Oh the wit!
LOUISE:	As I said just concentrate on yourself.
GILLIAN:	Ah well you seem to do that enough yourself.
LOUISE:	That's my job.
GILLIAN:	To concentrate on yourself? Consistently yourself throughout this show? There are two of us in this piece.
LOUISE:	Not in this context. Right now, I'm teaching you and you're doing it very badly.
GILLIAN:	I thought I had an idea of what you're doing here and clearly I don't.
LOUISE:	No, clearly I am being misunderstood here.
GILLIAN:	Oh god, get the violin out. Oh Lou you're too nice to argue.
LOUISE:	I'm an intellectual arguer.
GILLIAN:	An intellectual arguer!!? No you're not!
LOUISE:	I am actually. Just because you don't understand me. Where are we going with this argument? Where is it leading?
GILLIAN:	Have we ever had an argument before?
LOUISE:	[*to audience*] When we first lived together, we had a thing about vitamins.
GILLIAN:	[*to audience*] Yes, she told me I was really unhealthy.

LOUISE: I said she'd have enough vitamins if she ate fruit and vegetables.

GILLIAN: I said I was healthy-ish.

LOUISE: And I said she wasn't.

GILLIAN: And so it went on.

LOUISE: You said "well I supplement with vitamins".

GILLIAN: And you said I wouldn't have to if I ate fruit and vegetables.

LOUISE: And I said to eat spinach. And for the next three days she was saying "do you want some spinach or do you want some multi-vitamins? I'm having a multi-vitamin".

GILLIAN: We had an argument the other day during rehearsals.

LOUISE: She said on the phone, "well I can't rehearse Act 3 because I don't have my script".

GILLIAN: "I don't have my script, somebody's got it".

LOUISE: "It's in *my* bag but *I* didn't pack my bag". If I had I would have made sure, I'd have checked I had the right one.

GILLIAN: So I made the error, yes? "So will I come over and get it or are you in the bath?" (She's always in the bath).

LOUISE: Up to you. Just so long as you know I'm not trying to sabotage your script learning.

GILLIAN: I know you didn't do it on purpose, if I'd known I would have counted each script page out individually and anyway I didn't ring you to make issue with not having Act 3 coz I didn't even know that yet, I wanted to talk about Act 1.

LOUISE: That's just like you, you never bloody check anything.

GILLIAN: Give me strength. She's doing my head in.

LOUISE: Yes just shake off all responsibility.

GILLIAN: Who's the one making the big deal out of me not having Act 3? You're the one checking up on me all the time like I'm a four-year-old.

LOUISE: So, we turn up to rehearsal tomorrow and you say "I couldn't learn Act 3 coz it was in Lou's bag". I can just imagine what you'd say.

GILLIAN: Well obviously you were wrong.

LOUISE: Obviously. And another thing. When you've finished with my jacket that you've had for three months, I'd quite like it back.

GILLIAN: If you hadn't left it in my boot then …

LOUISE: Oh so it magically flew up from out of your car boot up three flights of stairs into your bedroom?

GILLIAN: Fine, if you want to be the nice one, you be the nice one, I'll be the freaky fucker. You've won.

LOUISE: Sod off Gillian.

[*Pause as both return to their seats and drink.*]

GILLIAN: I suppose it's all a rehearsal from the moment you get an idea and you speak it aloud or you get it down on paper and you keep on coming back to it again and again and again so the process, getting it right, I suppose that's a rehearsal. And you mock it up and each time you make it, it gets a little bit better, a little bit better, and you use the right material and get the fit right. I suppose if that's a rehearsal then yeah, I suppose you do what you're doing now, watch people piecing it together and start piecing it together, making connections, looking at the music you're going to use: "Live Forever" by Oasis, the words. Yeah I suppose it *is* a rehearsal, a rehearsal for that one moment that lasts for just a moment … [*laughs*] and then it's all gone forever.

Act 5: Playing Dead

GILLIAN: I've killed someone and I've got them buried under the patio.

LOUISE: I'm trapped underground, not able to move but still alive, buried alive.

GILLIAN: I'm trying to dig her out with my hands that are bleeding and my nails that are split.

LOUISE: There's a man in the shadows. I can't see his face. He's holding a gun, though I can't see it. He shoots me as I turn away.

GILLIAN: I'm held underwater by a stranger who is wearing a blue swatch watch and smells of tobacco.

LOUISE: It's late at night and someone is following me home, someone I can't see but I can hear his footsteps. As I turn the corner, he's touching me, holding my arms behind my back and pushing me to the ground, a long knife stuck through my ribs, all the way through to the back.

GILLIAN: It's Christmas morning. I'm four years old. I come downstairs early. Father Christmas is still in the living room. He turns round and I see he is holding a gun, his finger on the trigger.

LOUISE: I'm alone, probably in a horror movie of some kind, and I'm swept into the air, whisked out of the window and dropped twelve floors onto the concrete ground below.

GILLIAN: I invent, so that they do not happen, the most gruesome details. The door opens and an old man with a white beard pats me on the head. Sticks a gun to my back and shoots me.

LOUISE: Two strangers enter the room with revolvers or they attack me as I leave the theatre or they wait for me in the bar after rehearsals and seem not to recognise me. They take a revolver from their pocket and open fire on me.

GILLIAN: A group of terrorists surround my house on the hill. They crawl on their bellies and force their way into the house and up the stairs where one by one they take out the sleeping members of my family.

LOUISE: The presence of strangers scares me. Hidden behind their bottles of beer, vigilant, motionless and patient, watching me and waiting. Hiding under a table in the bar, flat on my stomach, facing the only door in the room. The door opens in front of me. There is an old man with a white beard, he pats me on the head and asks me how I am. Sticks a gun to my back and shoots me.

GILLIAN: Towards dawn I dream I am in a library. A librarian wearing dark glasses asks me what I'm looking for? I panic and start to run, she shoots me in the back.

LOUISE: A small room, such a small room, with doors side by side where walls should be, just doors. The doors are white. The floor is black. Two strangers enter the room with revolvers or attack me as I leave the theatre or wait for me inside the bar.

GILLIAN: The door opens in front of me. There is an old man with a white beard, he pats me on the head and asks me how I am. Sticks a gun to my back and shoots me.

LOUISE: The door opens behind me. I cannot see the man, but I can hear that he is wearing a plastic Mac. I can hear him fumbling with something. A gun. Two shots to the head, one to the chest.

GILLIAN: I'm in the corner of a room facing a brick wall (the corner where the two walls meet). The bricks are old and damp. I am out of breath and nervous, waiting for whoever is upstairs to come down, and I know it's just a matter of time …

LOUISE: I am sitting in a room, a really small room. I can walk five paces to one corner of the room and another five to get to the next corner. The walls are white. The floor is black. I'm sitting in the corner. I don't know whether someone will come and get me.

GILLIAN: I roll a cigarette from my pocket, I light it but do not smoke it as my hands are shaking and I imagine the light is failing and I am already dead.

LOUISE: A small man with no hair and a green coat enters the room, he asks "where are you?" I reply "in a room, a small room. The walls are white. The floor is black". At that moment I hear the sound of gun fire.

GILLIAN: I am sitting in a very small pink room surrounded by Christmas presents. I don't know how long I have been here, but I have just woken from a bad dream. I hear a knock on the door and Father Christmas walks in. He sits down next to me and I look into a mirror and see the face of a four-year-old. I turn to Father Christmas and he has a toy gun aimed at my head.

LOUISE: No matter how hard I run or jump or fall I still am stuck in the same spot. There are pins and needles in my right foot and I have an overwhelming taste of coffee in my mouth. As I recognise the taste, it changes to black tobacco.

GILLIAN: I see the shimmer of the blade as it fast approaches my eye. It plunges through the soft watery flesh and cracks through the bone behind.

LOUISE: I am lying dead in the lift, my bones broken and contorted, in a pool of my own blood and urine. The only clues to my murder are the diagrams scrawled across my body. [*Louise has been using makeup throughout this scene to draw strange diagrams over her body – She holds her arms out to show the audience.*]

GILLIAN: [*Gillian enacts the following text as a physical choreography – We recognise it from previous rehearsed choreographies*]. I am waiting. The strangers laugh loudly at me. They come closer and push me into the wall, they are laughing in my face, on and on and on. Each has a knife in their hand and they stab me one by one, my arms, my legs, my belly, my chest, my neck, my face. I try to scream but I can't. I try to run but I can't. A stranger arrives. I think he will save me, but he gets out a gun and shoots me in the stomach.

LOUISE: [*Louise enacts the following physically – She stands, gestures and turns face to the wall – Again we recognise this gestural motif from previous rehearsed choreographies*]. With a gesture, I ask the strangers to wait and turn to face the wall. I close my eyes and imagine that I am dreaming, that they will shoot me in the stomach, and that as the bullet enters my flesh I will wake up …

LOUISE: [*clicks*] I forgot my line. Can you give me my line? Page 168.

PROMPT: Oh yes. It's just … it really reminded me of something.

LOUISE: Oh does it? Are you sure?

PROMPT: It really reminded me of something … European, it's just quite quirky and dark.

LOUISE: I thought that we'd already done that bit. Have we missed a section?

Figure 15: Gillian eats her script in *Happy Hour*
(photo: Brian Slater).

Figure 16: Louise positions Old Man 1 for Ending 2 in *Happy Hour* (photo: Brian Slater).

PROMPT: I don't think either of you have been wholly accurate but …

LOUISE: OK OK. Perhaps it's time we were off-script now anyway Gill?

[Gillian and Louise begin to tear up their scripts and eat them – They retch throughout the sequence, as they improvise before the audience what is required in the making of a show – e.g. a beginning, a rehearsal space, lots of water, ideas, a director, a middle, taking risks, experimenting, repeating, warnings (don't work with children or animals, don't say 'Macbeth', don't 'whistle' etc.), and an ending…]

Act 6: Endings

[*depends on what audience voted for earlier*]

Ending 1:

[*Louise dances as Gillian holds a toy gun to her head.*]

Ending 2:

[*Gillian receives phone call, as Louise lies dead on the floor, Old Man 1 (in Father Christmas beard) pointing a toy gun at her.*]

THE END

Chapter 4 (Endings)

Death Becomes Us

Alan Fair

To speculate

What do we speak of when we speak of death?
Death stains us.
Death (su)stains us.

Each day I enter the ritualistic space of the public sphere, each day I am called upon to perform my identity, to demand of others and to be the subject of others' demands, to attest to the reality of suppositions about who I am and who the other is.

The performative, in this sense then, becomes like a symptom of something, but the something may just be the effect of the symptom, not something a priori to it but rather the imaginary signified of the signifier 'Act'. We bring about ourselves in the struggle to do so, not in the accurate delineation of a sense of being but rather in the fumbling that reminds us that the space of being is no place at all. This is what I see going on in Anna Fenemore's practice, the interrogation of the inter-act-ion between humans. The drama of acts, bodily acts, speech acts; the rhetoric of action, of bodies moving in social environments, bodies involved in social intercourse; drinking, chatting, and getting ready, seeking out in the other the response to their own truths, for truth, it seems, is a possibility.

Our experience of death is a form of the uncanny. A child is born and despite evidence to the contrary, it seems like a 'miracle'. Death, on the other hand, something as likely to happen as birth, and often with all the intimations, physical and otherwise, is often experienced as both an inevitability and a shocking circumstance. How does this 'tragedy' produce the drama of an ending?

We humans share this planet with many other living things and, it seems, we preoccupy ourselves with distinguishing humanity from these other creatures: we tell jokes, although the joke is on us, we laugh, although those others that share the sphere may one day get the last one … and we tell stories. I don't know if animals have the capacity to spin a yarn, except in the literal sense, I suspect they don't. Now, if you think about it, we are able to tell stories because of a salient feature of our consciousness, we are aware that we will, eventually, die.

Our awareness of dying allows us to structure the story in a particular way. Usually speaking we like to construct the fabula by means of beginnings, middles and ends. At first glimpse it may look like we start with the beginning but is it not the case that this starting point is always preceded by a sense of an ending or even 'The' ending?

We recognise that all 'this' must end and as a consequence we are able to construct the first two parts of the paradigm.

An ordinary man, John Smith, leads an uneventful life; he works as an office clerk in an anonymous building in the centre of the city. Every day he leaves his ordinary suburban house and his suburban wife and his suburban children and travels on the commuter train to work, a man, as they say, of no consequence; he votes with the majority and eats in the canteen with the other clerks, most of whom live in similar houses and have similar wives and similar children. One day John Smith takes a gun to work and kills twelve of his fellow workers and then commits suicide. Now the ordinary man's life must be inspected, clues must be found, reasons established. It is the endings that produce meanings. From this point on John Smith's horizon we are able to establish a narrative, structure meaning, are able to offer something like a reason for the unreasonable actions of a reasonable man.

Our instinct, then, is to tell stories, not just to make up stories but to repeat them, and this compulsion to repeat is something that, for Freud at least, lies at the heart of the beyond of the pleasure principle. Despite a residual optimism that Freud possessed regarding the organism, that what drives us is our seeking pleasure, there were just too many examples of a contrary trajectory, a trajectory that led him to speculate that there was something other than the instinct he labelled Eros. This aspect of the human condition seemed to exist not as a sole principle but as one aspect of a dialectic, the other being Thanatos.

There is a moment in Joseph H. Lewis's (1955) noir masterwork, *The Big Combo* when the two main protagonists, a cop (Mr Diamond) and a hoodlum (Mr Brown) (the law and its opposition), discuss a woman, a woman (Miss Lowell) they both want to possess, a woman (Jean Wallace) who, of course, defines them. The cop is played by Cornel Wilde, the criminal is here played by Richard Conte. Conte is perfectly cast, endowed as he is with a certain graceful narcissism. In the dark penumbrated room represented by canted angles and brooding shot/reverse shot they discuss the woman and their feelings towards her; Wilde moves to show sympathy with his nemesis, "I know how you feel" he offers. Conte looks at him, a wry movement in his eyes, studying the figure of the cop he replies, "No you don't. Nobody knows how someone else feels".

This moment rings both in and out of context as a kind of horrible truth. Here the mobster speaks with what at first might seem cynicism towards the possibility of understanding. We are all trapped inside ourselves, assuming, that is, that there is an inside. Maybe no one knows how someone else feels because, generally speaking, we tend to think of feelings and emotions as things that happen on our insides. There are of course the manifestations written on the body, tears and laughter, wringing hands and agitated head movements. Maybe Wilde might have said "I recognise your situation" or "I can see how you are acting". And it is this dilemma that we elaborate on in our everyday lives, the search to express ourselves and to seek out the expression of self in others, a mutual dependence of (non) intimacy. Speech personifies this inward externalisation: the 'extimate'. This Lacanian neologism functions as a report on the situation we find ourselves in, conceiving of self as inside while constantly seeking ways to be outside, to, as it were, express ourselves. The voice both emanates from the inside, the intimate, and expresses itself on the outside, the external. It is as though our bodies were the liminal site of experience, somewhere between the social and the psychological, the internal and the external, the space between two abstractions given solidity by this translating medium. The body, my body, affords this translation; here the body is the locus whereby 'I' becomes 'me' where 'me' becomes 'Alan', the one who is deemed a subject.

So the dialogue is the ritual of expressing a supposed interior that may be signified but not known, not grasped as such. The act of speech is the act of figuration; the human figure conjures up itself as being in the process of vanishing, of dying.

I imagine your death, I imagine my death, not as a wilful act but as a bulwark against the event; discourse allows me to exist. In this drama, this exchange of words offers ourselves time to address mortality, and in the dialogue played out as drama something is offered to the spectators, the audience. By enacting dialogues concerning death we open the space for a specific interaction, one that assumes the generality of mortality and the specificity of mortal thoughts. What are the special circumstances by which we enable ourselves to speak of death?

The body is stained by the mark of this recognition, a stain that is shared amongst bodies, bodies that know, bodies of knowledge, the certain assurance of the stains signifying property. Through speech we allow the stain to appear in the midst of theatre, an enactment is shared between the communities, a form arises, a form of narration: beginning – middle – end. And the end may be surmised as form but also outside form and that is why we must rehearse the event. Our experience of the event can only function as an indexical sign, not of what has been but of what will (certainly) be. Death becomes us, we become death, the appearance and disappearance is the play of these moments. Tell me your fantasy and I'll tell you mine and we will be none the wiser, for our wisdom is futile in the certainty, and maybe this is the secret of the exchange of words, the grammar of our emotions rehearsed as play. In each interchange the ludic is exposed; we are so serious about the manner in which we imagine, and can only imagine *as if* death were imaginary and not the real of our destiny.

Let me say here now, while the origins of the Universe are an almost obsessive trope in the physical sciences, that is to say, of humans, the universe itself is completely indifferent to it. For it is humans who care for beginnings, middles, ends and narratives, not the earth and the stars.

To see

The true barrier that holds the subject back in front of the unspeakable field of radical desire that is the field of absolute destruction, of destruction beyond putrefaction, is properly speaking the aesthetic phenomenon where it is identified with the experience of beauty – beauty in all its shining radiance, beauty that has been called the splendour of truth. It is obviously because truth is not pretty to look at that beauty is, if not its splendour, then at least its envelope.

(Lacan, 2006: 217)

We might say that Christianity is itself an eastern Mediterranean death cult – Christ on the cross – we look up at his defiled body and quake with fear. Christ's body laid out, we look down and in his death realise not just the death of the other but also the life of ourselves; Christians celebrate the death of Christ as a form of affirmation of life: he dies so that we might live. The image of death, a word, a painting, a sculpture brings us through the signifier closer to our lives, we are mortal, and mortality is the destiny of not just the body but also the self:

The self eroticizes and signifies the obsessive presence of Death by stamping with isolation, emptiness, or absurd laughter its own imaginative assurance that keeps it alive, that is, anchored in the interplay of forms. To the contrary, images and identities – the carbon copies of that triumphant self – are imprinted with inaccessible sadness.

(Kristeva, 1989: 138)

If you happen to find yourself in the Italian city of Napoli, you may stroll along that most carnivalesque of all thoroughfares the Spaccanapoli, also known as via Benedetto Croce. Here, almost opposite the street shrine to the footballer Maradona, you will come across the modest entrance to the Capella Sansevero. Upon entering you are confronted, this is the right word, with a figure rendered in marble, the figure is of the dead Christ, a body laid out on a plinth and covered by a veil. The piece is, not unsurprisingly, known as *The Veiled Christ*. It is stunning. The work was conceived of, initially, by the Venetian artist Antonio Corradini, but in fact was executed by Giuseppe Sanmartino, a native of Napoli.

What strikes the viewer when first encountering this baroque marvel is the extreme sense of layers, of a veil literally draped over the body as though the artist had first hewn the facsimile of the dead body and then carved the simulation of the fine covering, its folds and ripples seemingly clinging to the abjected body. This act of representation is not only marvellous, it is also instructional. The piece that we gaze upon perfectly accomplishes the idea of the exterior.

The body lies on a plinth that is below eye level, we are caused to look down, to see the body from above. Our relationship to this form is base, we no longer look upward at the crucifixion but cast our eyes down. With downcast eyes the illusion assumes a mournful spectacle; our wonder is tinged by the sight of death, as bodies we move from the horizontal to the vertical and back again. We look at the veil as separate from something that lies beneath it when this is clearly not the case. There is, in truth, no underneath. This figure, emaciated, lifeless underneath the veil is, in fact, the illusion. The body and its covering are all of a piece. There is no underneath; there is only the effect of something there. Isn't this the way we assume the interior, the underneath of our own bodies? Beneath the veil of our skins, our tissue is where our 'true' self can be found, "the real me", the me who, as it were, transcends the limits of this social self, the self that is the act, an act that is always concealing an essence. The Sanmartino sculpture enacts this drama of the extimate, this revelation as trompe l'oeil.

This is not all the chapel has to offer. In the same room there is another statue, this time not one we gaze down upon, but one raised on a plinth so that we crane our necks upward towards its demands. This figure is another veiled body, this time of a full-breasted woman. This sculpture is called 'Chastity' or otherwise, 'Modesty'. The effect is the same; the veil has the appearance of covering the naked body 'beneath'. The figure rendered by Corradini not only functions in the same manner, to confound the logic of our gaze, but something else occurs here, for when we discover the title for the creation we are immediately struck by the ambiguity of the title. Is it the body that is covered as an act of modesty or is the title addressed to the viewer, is it our modesty that is addressed? Am I to be kept safe from a revelation by my own modesty? The sculpture allows me to look without the contamination, the stain of a blush. This statue, still and silent, seeks to animate me and yet wishes to produce a mask of respectability. As in the drama, I am allowed licence to see, to become part of the gaze that envelops us all in the performance of our respective positions. Our upward gaze demands another position, a radical re-alignment with the observed figure, no longer base but elevated.

Just as in the process of drama the question of the address is rendered problematic. When the actors address each other as characters, where does the drama lie? In the act? In the body of the actors? In the reception of the audience? The veil of acting, of enactment, is the treachery of the Sanmartino marble, the Corradini woman. We are asked to participate in the drama of a supposed interior that itself is a cloak. Incidentally, the position of the actors here, between viewer and viewed, becomes a complex series of negotiations. Do we look down from the balcony, up from the stalls, or as is the case in *The Rehearsal (a trilogy)*, do we look directly at the actors directly next to us? Is the sight line a part of the dramatic experience?

177

To spectate

Rancière, in his essay "The Emancipated Spectator" tells us that,

> [w]hat is required is a theatre without spectators, where those in attendance learn from as opposed to being seduced by images; where they become active participants as opposed to passive voyeurs.

> (Rancière, 2009: 4)

First one must observe in Rancière's polemic that there is an assumption that the spectator is in need of emancipation, that the spectator is to be liberated from her passivity. He argues that the playwright/director, "knows that she must do one thing – overcome the gulf separating activity from passivity" (2009: 12).

Emancipation, he goes on,

> begins when we challenge the opposition between viewing and acting; when we understand that the self-evident facts that structure the relations between saying, seeing and doing themselves belong to the structure of domination and subjection. It begins when we understand that viewing is also an action that confirms or transforms this distribution of positions.

> (Rancière, 2009: 13)

It is in the intimate architecture of Fenemore's work that this distribution of positions is enabled. The drama is integrated into the space, performance here, in a pub(lic) bar, is accomplished by the actors and audience/spectators. The senses are imbricated into the moment, body movements, the smell of sweat, the reek of alcohol, the embarrassment of intimacy, all of this is what *The Rehearsal (a trilogy)* seeks to engage with. By staging the dialogue between actants, we liberate language, the dialogic of artistic speech fills the dramatic space and is, therefore, emancipatory in the shared space of the drama. There is, in this sense, no them and us, no me and you, only the hopeless realisation of the community enacted.

The concern to stage is not the same as the stage, here the redistribution of knowledges are meant to produce the shared experience, what Rancière calls a "new intellectual adventure" (2009: 15). Adventuresome drama, antic, ludic, the pleasures of death as Ragland might name it. The collective experiences the space through which the dialogue courses as a new form, a new idiom as a medium for the expression of this tangible dialectic, no audience, no performers or more properly all audience, all performers. This is the shared drama of our collective understanding that death and speech are inextricably linked in our consciousness of self and in the political unconscious of a new enactment.

To cite

We live our lives in generalities and remember them in specifics. Memory arranges us into ourselves, the stories we tell. In his essay "The Story Teller" Walter Benjamin, in section ten of the piece, writes about the relationship between the process of the story teller and death. He argues that we have ostracised death; "dying has been pushed further and further out of the perceptual world of the living" (Benjamin, 1992: 93). He argues that the space of death is no longer the space of the domestic and that we have become, in a memorable phrase, "dry dwellers of eternity" (Benjamin, 1992: 93). His argument is that the proximity of death is, at the least, a source of our ability to tell tales.

It is this sociability of death that I see as part of *The Rehearsal (a trilogy)*, this bringing back the proximate, the domestic aspect of our relationship between the discourses and the actualities of death and dying.

> Does Holbein forsake us, as Christ, for an instant, had imagined himself forsaken? Or does he, on the contrary, invite us to change the Christly tomb into a living tomb, to participate in the painted death and thus include it in our life, in order to live with it and make it live? For if the living body, in opposition to the rigid corpse, is a dancing body, doesn't our life, through an identification with death, become a Danse Macabre in keeping with Holbein's other well-known depiction?

> (Kristeva, 1989: 113–4)

A drive, Freud held, is "an urge inherent in organic life to restore an earlier state of things" (Freud, 1920: 36). And as this organic precedes the inorganic, "the aim of all life" he concluded in a famous phrase

> "is death" … As the formula "an urge inherent in organic life" suggests, the death drive may not be beyond the pleasure principle but rather anterior to it: dissolution comes before binding – at the level of the cell as well as of the ego. In this sense the death drive may be the foundation rather than the exception of the pleasure principle, which may indeed "serve" it.

> (Foster, 1995: 10–11)

In this sense there is indeed life after death, this is it, we live our lives after, not before, this dissolution. Thus we strive in some ways to cover over this possibility of dissolution through what we might call symbolic forms – stories for example. Here is how Ragland in her discussion of Lacan's reading of the Freudian death drive has it:

> A palpable void lies at the heart of language, being and body. Thus, it is loss that drives life, making of the death drive a matter of clinging to known consistencies rather than encountering the unbearable real of loss qua anxiety. The object 'a' denotes any filler of this void. As such, it quickly grounds being in repetitions – repeating relations to objects whose crucial function of semblance is that of filling up an actual void … Repetitious rituals become habits, turning Eros into Thanatos. Even though repetition is not inherently lethal, it attaches us to stasis by invisible bonds.

> (Ragland, 1994: 87)

The rituals of telling stories, of rehearsing ways to complete narratives, of finding ways to come to an end – these activities all introduce death into discourse and at the same time seek to repress it. Absence is revealed and compensated for. Let us consider Freud's observation of the child's game 'Fort/Da': the game itself is a form of narrative; first something appears then it disappears only to re-appear. In this game, the child's anxiety at the loss of the mother (she leaves the room) is overcome by the symbolic form. A cotton reel is attached to some cotton; the reel is thrown out of sight and then retrieved by means of the thread. What is important is not that the child has power over the object but that the object's actuality is marked by language. It is the words that seem to offer the jubilant overcoming of loss even as they enact it. How many of us have observed and even played the game with a child who throws something from a pushchair only to squeal with delight when the adult returns it. By speaking of absence (death?) are we not all children? This pleasure that a child expresses is obtained, maybe, through a curious relationship with death and repetition. Ragland again:

> Pleasure turns to displeasure because repetition, by definition, refers to a preceding moment – to the loss of a pleasure (or consistency). The pleasure remains, however, as a fixation, a trace (or "letter") in memory, and gives body to fantasy. Thus, pleasure is retrieved via repetition that constitutes fantasies of eradicating loss.

> (Ragland, 1994: 89)

The real (reel?) of anxiety is allayed by the field of language, language that is very often transformed in ritual. We ask ourselves who we are, or more properly, how are we perceived? What is it that I lack? A lack that structures me because I must encounter this lack in order to ask the question, to ask the question of an other, to enter into a dialogue with the other both 'out there' and 'in here'.

So if we are in this world that Benjamin described nearly eight decades ago, a place where society has effectively banished death, how are we to rehearse the situation? Strangely, we often, in response to actual death, exclaim that it "was like being in a movie". As Gillian says in *Happy Hour*, "but there's something about when those real experiences happen that you think it's not happening to you, it's happening to someone else, or you're in a film, or you're in a play". We encounter this very real moment as though it were a fiction, something made-up, a fantasy. This real is what we cannot seem to access; it seems that this encounter is a kind of de-realisation, that there, in a sense, can be no real of me. As Martin says in *Death Rattle*: "You have an accident and you lose your memory. That is one of the manifestations of the real, in other words the real is trauma, and trauma is so much not part of our everyday lives so we say it's like in the movies". Or as Freud writes:

> Our own death is indeed quite unimaginable, and whenever we make the attempt to imagine it we … really survive as spectators … At bottom nobody believes in his own death, or to put the same thing in a different way, in the unconscious every one of us is convinced of his own immortality.

(Freud, 1953: 304–5)

Where is this real me, inside me, in my vital organs, my brain, my mind? If it comes to that, where is mind? Maybe we might be able to understand mind as something that occurs *between* us rather than *in* us. That the real of each of us is in the process of our coming together? Exactly the coming together of us as audience/spectators and players, in a fiction if you like, but nevertheless a fiction that allows us to catch a glimpse of the real of ourselves and the reality of social being. If the knowable world seemed to be slipping away from Benjamin and his culture when he wrote "The Story Teller" in 1935, how much more has it slipped away now? Shifted into the ether of the worldwide web, the reality of our finitude is more than ever a kind of dream. Death becomes us, but what of our avatars?

The Rehearsal (a trilogy) based on interviews with...

Louise Bennett

Teresa Brayshaw

Jon Brazil

Martin Buchan

Peter Crory

Olive Denneny

Alan Fair

Anna Fenemore

Kate Fenemore

John Franklin

Amanda Griffkin

Shirley Harrington

Dorothy Haugh

Peter Kennedy

183

Shane Kinghorn

Gillian Knox

Irene Knox

Uel Knox

Dick McCaw

Neil Mackenzie

Lorraine McFarland

Paul Makin

Josh Moran

Arthur Pritchard

Jonathan Taylor

Wendy Valentine

(and 23 other contributors who prefer not to be named.)

With script contributions for Part 1: *Death Rattle* from Anna Barzotti and Jim Hinks.

With thanks to you all.

Bibliography

Ackerman, D. (1999), *Deep Play*, New York: Vintage Books.

Bajekal, M. (2002), *Health Survey for England 2000: Care Homes and Their Residents*, London: The Stationery Office.

Barba, E. and Savarese, N. (1991), *The Secret Art of the Performer: A Dictionary of Theatre Anthropology*, London: Routledge.

Becker, E. (1972), *The Birth and Death of Meaning*, Harmondsworth: Penguin.

Becker, E. (1973), *The Denial of Death*, New York: Free Press.

Benjamin, W. (1992), *Illuminations*, London: Fontana Press

Booth, T. (1985), *Home Truths: Old People's Homes and the Outcomes of Care*, Aldershot, Hants: Gower Publishing Company.

Bowker, J. (1991), *The Meanings of Death*, Cambridge: Cambridge University Press.

Caillois, R. (2001), *Man, Play and Games*, Urbana and Chicago: University of Illinois Press.

Couliano, I. P. (1991), *Out of This World: Otherworld Journeys from Gilgamesh to Albert Einstein*, London: Shambala.

De Certeau, M. (1984), *The Practice of Everyday Life*, Berkeley, Los Angeles and London: University of California Press.

De Certeau, M. (1985), "Practices of Space", in M. Blonsky (ed.), *On Signs*, Oxford: Basil Blackwell.

Deleuze, G. and Guattari, F. (1988), *A Thousand Plateaus: Capitalism and Schizophrenia*, London: The Athlone Press.

Department of Health (1999), *Community Care Statistics; Home Help: Home Care Services*, London: The Stationary Office.

Department of Health. (1990), *NHS and Community Care Act*, London: HMSO

DeVita, M. A. (2001), "The Death Watch: Certifying Death Using Cardiac Criteria", *Progress in Transplantation* 11 (1), pp. 58–66.

Douglas, M. (1984), *Purity and Danger: An Analysis of the Concepts of Pollution and Taboo*, London: Routledge and Kegan Paul.

Dydo, U. E. (2003), *Gertrude Stein: The Language that Rises: 1923–1934*, Illinois: Northwestern University Press.

Earle, S., Komaromy, C. and Bartholomew, C. (eds) (2008), *Death and Dying: A Reader*, London: Sage.

Earle, S., Komaromy, C. and Bartholomew, C. (eds) (2009), *Making Sense of Death, Dying and Bereavement: An Anthology*, London: Sage.

Etchells, T. (1999), *Certain Fragments: Contemporary Performance and Forced Entertainment*, London: Routledge.

Foster, H. (1995), *Compulsive Beauty*, Cambridge, MA and London: MIT Press.

Frankenheimer, J. (dir) (1962) *Birdman of Alcatraz*, [film], USA: Norma Productions.

Frazer, J. G. (1913), *The Belief in Immortality and the Worship of the Dead*, Vols 1–3, London: Dawsons of Pall Mall.

Freud, S. (1920), *Beyond the Pleasure Principle*, London: Hogarth Press.

Freud, S. (1953), "Thoughts for the Times on War and Death", *The Standard Edition of the Complete Psychological Works of Sigmund Freud*, Vol. 4, London: Hogarth Press.

Garner, S. B. (1994), *Bodied Spaces: Phenomenology and Performance in Contemporary Drama*, New York: Cornell University Press.

Goffman, E. (1959), *The Presentation of Self in Everyday Life*, London: Penguin.

Goffman, E. (1961), *Asylums*, London: Penguin.

Helmer, J. and Malzacher, F. (eds) (2004), *Not Even a Game Anymore: The Theatre of Forced Entertainment*, Berlin: Alexander Verlag.

Hind, C. (2010), "Dark and Deep Play in Performance Practice", unpublished Ph.D. thesis, University of Leeds.

Hochschild, A. R. (1983), *The Managed Heart: The Commercialization of Human Feeling*, Berkley, CA: University of California Press.

Hockey, J., Komaromy, C. and Woodthorpe, K. (2010), *The Matter of Death: Space, Place and Materiality*, Hampshire: Palgrave Macmillan.

Holden, J., Greyson, B. and James, D. (eds) (2009), *The Handbook of Near-Death Experiences: Thirty Years of Investigation*, Santa Barbara, CA: ABC-CLIO.

Howarth, G. (2007), *Death and Dying: A Sociological Introduction*, Cambridge: Polity.

Jay, M. (1993), "Sartre, Merleau-Ponty, and the Search for a New Ontology of Sight", in D. M. Levin (ed.), *Modernity and the Hegemony of Vision*, Berkeley, CA and London: University of California Press.

Jenks, C. (ed.) (1995), *Visual Culture*, London: Routledge.

Kellehear, A. (1996), *Experiences Near Death: Beyond Medicine and Religion*, New York: Oxford University Press.

Kellehear, A. (2000), *Eternity and Me: The Everlasting Things in Everyday Life*, Melbourne: Hill of Content.

Kellehear, A. (2007), *A Social History of Dying*, Cambridge: Cambridge University Press.

Knudsen, S. K. (2005), "A Review of the Criteria Used to Assess Insensibility and Death in Hunted Whales Compared to Other Species", *The Veterinary Journal* 169, pp. 42–59.

Komaromy, C. (2010), "Dying Spaces in Dying Places: Care Homes for Older Adults", in J. Hockey, C. Komaromy and K. Woodthorpe (eds), *The Matter of Death: Space, Place and Materiality*, Hampshire: Palgrave Macmillan.

Kristeva, J. (1989), *Black Sun: Depression and Melancholia*, New York and Chichester: Columbia University Press.

Lacan, J. (1992), *The Ethics of Psychoanalysis 1959–1960*, London: Routledge.

Lacan, J. (2006), *Écrits*, New York and London: Norton.

Lehrer, J. (2007), *Proust was a Neuroscientist*, Boston and New York: Houghton Miflin.

Lewis, J. H. (dir.) (1955), *The Big Combo*, [film], USA: Security Pictures and Theodora Productions.

Liechty, D. (ed.) (2002), *Death and Denial: Interdisciplinary Perspectives on the Legacy of Ernest Becker*, Westport, CT: Praeger.

Manning, P. (1992), *Erving Goffman and Modern Sociology*, Cambridge: Polity Press.

ONS (Office National Statistics) (2002), www.statistics.gov.uk (accessed 03/03/05).

Osis, K. and Haraldsson, E. (1977), *At the Hour of Our Death*, New York: Hastings House.

Page, S. and Komaromy, C. (2005), "Professional Performance: The Case of Expected and Unexpected Deaths", *Mortality*, November 2005, 10(4), pp. 294–307.

Quick, A. (2004), "Bloody Play", in J. Helmer and F. Malzacher (eds), *Not Even a Game Anymore: The Theatre of Forced Entertainment* (pp. 139–69), Berlin: Alexander Verlag.

Ragland, E. (1994), *Essays on the Pleasure of Death: From Freud to Lacan*, New York and London: Routledge.

Bibliography

Rancière, J. (2009), *The Emancipated Spectator*, London: Verso.

Schechner, R. (2002), *Performance Studies: An Introduction* Oxon and New York: Routledge.

Stacey, M. (1991), *The Sociology of Health and Healing*, London: Routledge.

Sudnow, D. (1967), *Passing On: The Social Organisation of Dying*, New Jersey: Prentice-Hall.

Timmermans, S. (1991), "When Death Isn't Dead: Implicit Social Rationing during Resuscitation Efforts", *Sociological Inquiry*, Vol. 69 (i), pp. 51–75.

Timmermans, S. (1998), "Resuscitation Technology in the Emergency Department: Towards a Dignified Death", *Sociology of Health and Illness*, 20 (2), pp. 144–67.

Townsend, P. (1962), *The Last Refuge: A Survey of Residential Institutions and Homes for the Aged in England and Wales*, London: Routledge & Kegan Paul.

Van Gennep, A. (1960), *The Rites of Passage*, London: Routledge & Kegan Paul.

Vitebsky, P. (1995), *The Shaman*, London: Duncan Beard Publishers.

Zaleski, C. (1987), *Otherworld Journeys: Accounts of Near-Death Experiences in Medieval and Modern Times*, New York: Oxford University Press.

Zarrilli, P. B. (ed.) (1995), *Acting (Re)Considered*, London and New York: Routledge.